The real labour is to remember, to attend.
In fact, to come awake. Still more, to remain awake.

C.S. LEWIS

Gregory Spencer

discernment

innocence

authenticity

awakening the

modesty

quieter virtues

reverence

contentment

generosity

IVP Books

An imprint of InterVarsity Press
Downers Grove, Illinois

InterVarsity Press
P.O. Box 1400, Downers Grove, IL 60515-1426
World Wide Web: www.ivpress.com
E-mail: email@ivpress.com

InterVarsity Press® is the book-publishing division of InterVarsity Christian Fellowship/USA®, a
movement of students and faculty active on campus at hundreds of universities, colleges and schools
of nursing in the United States of America, and a member movement of the International Fellowship
of Evangelical Students. For information about local and regional activities, write Public Relations
Dept., InterVarsity Christian Fellowship/USA, 6400 Schroeder Rd., P.O. Box 7895, Madison, WI
53707-7895, or visit the IVCF website at <www.intervarsity.org>.

All Scripture quotations, unless otherwise indicated, are taken from the Holy Bible, Today's New
International Version™ Copyright © 2001 by International Bible Society. All rights reserved.

Design: Cindy Kiple
Images: Thomas Northcut/Getty Images

ISBN 978-0-8308-3735-9

Printed in the United States of America ∞

Library of Congress Cataloging-in-Publication Data

Spencer, Gregory H. (Gregory Horton), 1953-
  Awakening the quieter virtues / Gregory Spencer.
      p. cm.
  Includes bibliographical references (p.   ).
  ISBN 978-0-8308-3735-9 (pbk.: alk. paper)
  1. Virtues. 2. Christian life. I. Title.
  BV4630.S64 2010
  241'.4—dc22
                                                              2010008455

P   18   17   16   15   14   13   12   11   10   9   8   7   6   5   4   3   2   1

Y   25   24   23   22   21   20   19   18   17   16   15   14   13   12   11   10

For my father,
Glenn Allen Spencer,
who modeled for me
hard work and attention to detail

and in memory of my mother,
Jane Ellen Spencer,
who loved to listen to
our stories

CONTENTS

Acknowledgments. 9

1 THE GRINCH WAS RIGHT 11

2 DISCERNMENT: Choosing Life or Cheering Death . 21
   The Discipline of Attentiveness

3 INNOCENCE: Lost and Found 44
   The Discipline of Advocacy

4 AUTHENTICITY: Our Genuine Longing 67
   The Discipline of Real Presence

5 MODESTY: It's Not a Modest Virtue 88
   The Discipline of Timely Remembrance

6 REVERENCE: The Church Without Shoes 109
   The Discipline of Astonishment

7 CONTENTMENT: Don't Care How; I Want It Now! . 132
   The Discipline of Ars Morendi

8 GENEROSITY: Fingers, Fists and an Open Hand. . . 156
   The Discipline of Compassionate Imagination

9 SHOUTING SOFTLY 181

Appendix: *Definitions and Disciplines*. 187

Notes 189

ACKNOWLEDGMENTS

Some writers go into their cubbyholes to compose, refine and then present their words in fairly finished form to the world. Then there are writers like me, folks who blurt out any new idea to anyone who will listen: colleagues across the hall, students in class, friends via e-mail or neighbors out walking their dogs. Consequently, my list of those to thank is quite long—and their responses to my blurtings have been full of wisdom.

At Westmont College, I have introduced many of this book's assertions in numerous media ethics classes. Thank you, students, for your indulgence and good advice.

Colleagues at Westmont have privileged me with one of the great blessings of academic life: stimulating and witty conversation. I'm grateful for the discourse of Mark Nelson, Jim Taylor, Ben Patterson, Bruce Fisk, Deborah Dunn, Lesa Stern and Omedi Ochieng.

Many students lovingly spent red ink on the book's behalf. Heaps of thanks to Emily Harms, Laurel Myers, Jon Saur, Jasmine Steller, Brittney Brown, Bethany Sie, Jessica Conrad, Maddy Weiss, Nancy Shieh, Alison Trowbridge, Rachel Fasig. I'm sure I'm missing a few more!

Other readers, Tim Eaton, Richard Curtis, Donna Speer and Charlotte DeVries, added sage counsel. Laura Wilson, my secretary for over two decades, typed and critiqued to good effect.

Special thanks to three who read the whole manuscript with shrewd eyes: Matt Smith, Emily Minor, June Michealson. Your efforts reformed the book!

I'm grateful for fellow parishioners at Montecito Covenant Church who cheered me on—and asked insightful questions that "just had to be answered."

Once again, Kirk and Bonnie Steele graciously loaned out their desert home for annual writing retreats—and thanks to my old pal Ken Kornelis who accompanies me. Your mind sharpens mine, and has done so for forty years.

Tim Beals of Credo Communication and Cindy Bunch at Inter-Varsity Press have kept the process going with encouragement and competence.

Most importantly, I thank my family, who inquired, emboldened and teased in love. A sigh and a swell of the heart to daughters Laura, Hannah and Emily (and her recently betrothed, Tim Stewart). And how can I say enough about my own betrothed? Janet, my dear, your character reveals more each day that I married "up." How would I have made it through without you?

1 ❧ THE GRINCH WAS RIGHT

How is it no one sees how deeply afraid we were, last night, this morning? Is it something we all hide from each other, by mutual consent?

DON DeLILLO

I awoke to the sound of gunfire. I lurched out of bed, grabbed my aching knees, threw on my robe and ran to the window. Would I see a police squad storming my neighbor's house or a psychopath aiming a rifle into the sky? Neither. There, in the driveway, a car backfired as the driver threw our newspaper onto the honeysuckle. I stumbled out the door, hoping no one would see my sleepy face and pale, skinny legs. Then I squinted down at the headlines: economic problems, terrorism, political wrangling and a sex scandal. Quickly, I moved to the sports page.

By the time I got back inside, the upstairs thumped to the beat of my daughters' music. Perhaps the car had awakened them as well. After a shower, a shave and breakfast, I completed ten minutes of "devotions," including twenty seconds of high-quality prayer. Then I checked my e-mail, called a business and got put on hold (while being assured that my call was valuable), played com-

puter solitaire to bide my time, checked e-mail again, heard the
microwave ding, took out my reheated coffee, checked e-mail
again, gave up on the phone call, kissed my wife goodbye, hopped
in the car and drove to a store.

As I raced through curves, radio announcers told me to buy a
lottery ticket, get tires at a discount and call in to win a free pass
to the latest movie. At the grocery store, I grabbed a "homemade"
lunch package, waited impatiently in the long line, heard the
"beeps" of the cashier's scanner, read outrageous headlines on the
tabloids, listened to music coming out of the earbuds of the guy in
front of me . . . and so on and so on.

Oh, the noise, noise, noise, noise.

On any given day, many of us would say that Dr. Seuss's Grinch
was right. Every Who down in Whoville sings for our attention
and money, and we get fed up. We scream from our caves that we
are going to unplug once and for all . . . then we turn up the volume of our favorite rock songs, and the world is put right again.

OUR DAILY CACOPHONY

In our times, noise is inescapable—and it includes more than
sound. *Noise could be understood as everything that clamors for our
attention.* Of course, there is physical noise, such as the hum of the
freeway or the incessant meowing of my elderly cat. But we hear
other sounds as well: noises about how to live, what is important
and who we need to be.

Noise is not evil. Some noises we can control; some we cannot.
Some we ignore; others drive us crazy. And some sounds get into
our heads and motivate our actions.

Physical noise. We don't need to be convinced that the world is
noisy to our ears. We hear cars, trains and planes. Washers, vacu-
ums, fans. Screaming kids. At a recent college football game I attended, the sound system blasted deafeningly whenever the game
stopped: advertisements, announcements, pounding music that

made conversation impossible. Silence was not to be tolerated.

There are also physical noises that don't come at the ear, but at the eye. We live in an image-saturated world, a world that shouts at us visually. From TV, the Internet, movies and magazines, this blitz of images flashes by at a rate too speedy to process rationally, and it often moves us to overstate the photographic values of beauty, artistic composition, flashiness, violence and newness.

Todd Gitlin describes what it's like to live in a constant flow of images. He says that as we watch, "something *feels* uniform—a relentless pace, a pattern of interruption, a pressure toward unseriousness, a readiness for sensation, an anticipation of the next new thing." We can't help but be attracted to the liveliness of images, their beauty and stimulation, so much so that our desire may grow into an addiction, a need to feel the qualities Gitlin lists—qualities that make for breezy, shallow, unconnected experience. We flit around, treating life like a series of snapshots. Sometimes we are amazed by images, sometimes dulled. We may close our eyes for relief, but usually not for long.

Cultural noise. Contemporary America sends us thousands of messages a day, from "Get the body you always wanted" to "Don't miss this movie's exciting bloodbath." Our glamour-conscious society tells us to do what it takes to be and stay beautiful, rich, young and famous. All of this requires *more:* more sexiness, more consumer goods, more twentysomethingness, more popularity. Conveniently, all of these are available for purchase.

Another loud message is that freedom of choice is a value of supreme importance. The whole point of having an enviable appearance and the right amount of wealth is that we will then be able to do as we please, like celebrities do. Choose your dream vacation. Choose a self-serving moral system. According to our culture, freedom is important because with it we can have more fun, and more fun is, well, more fun than we are currently having. And if fun is the purpose of life, we should have *extreme* fun.

Snowboard off a cliff! Rent a Bugatti speedster for a day! Make love for ten hours straight! Why have ordinary fun when we can have an epic experience?

Our culture also tells us that faster is better. Impatiently, we shout "C'mon!" to our lazy microwave. Or we raise our hands in frustration as our computer takes "so long" to complete a task. One of my pet peeves is the Freeway Lane Darter, the driver who, no matter how heavy the traffic, races by on my right and then cuts in front of me. "Congratulations!" I yell. "You will now arrive at your destination one second sooner!" The faster we go, the more our peripheral vision begins to blur. Carl Honoré's *In Praise of Slowness* offers a correction: "instead of doing everything faster, do everything at the right speed." What are we missing? We will have to slow down if we want to pose that question.

Curiously, while we are trying to live the message that everything matters *now*, we are also told that nothing *really* matters. There is no Certain Truth, no transcendent reality. Since all is opinion and feeling, the best we can do is find some pleasure in the moment, some diversion from our troubles. Maybe we can make a difference here and there—but most of the time, we contend with the paradoxical sounds of the noise of everythingness and the noise of nothingness. We are overwhelmed with stimulation, but we are often left feeling empty.

Emotional noise. Our memory can loudly replay events we wish had never occurred. Sexual abuse, parenting mistakes, estrangement from friends. And most of us hear accusing voices that tell us we don't measure up. I went to an "accelerated" summer school after sixth grade. One day, my teacher, the thoroughly science-oriented Mrs. R, took me aside and said, "Greg, I don't think you belong here." Since my aptitudes were not in science, she was probably right, but I took her statement to mean that I did not belong, that I was an intellectual lightweight or, horror of horrors, merely average. We all hear voices from our past, voices that say we are deficient, that we will never amount to anything.

Some noises lead to persistent doubt or despair. I'll never forget when the phone rang, and I heard the words "We lost Joe." A good friend of mine—a church leader, a terrific family man—had committed suicide. I felt shock, heartache and guilt. How could this happen? How could he leave his family, friends, life itself, all because of imploding finances? And what does his choice say about God's effectiveness as healer, refuge, sovereign Lord? Try as I might, I can't explain the complexities of this man's collapse. His death clangs around in my head.

We also hear naggingly loud questions about the future. Will I be able to get a good job and keep it? Will I ever get married or stay married or have kids or raise them well? Will I fulfill my dreams? Will I fulfill my parents' dreams? Will the earth survive, or will we survive what is happening to the earth? Will anyone ever love me fully? Will I know God or stay faithful to him? What if I never get better than I am right now? What will happen when I die? Sometimes we suppress these questions; sometimes we face them well. If not addressed, these noises can shout down our spirit and stunt our growth. They can damage our ability to hear God's voice.

DEAFENING NOISE AND DEAFNESS

According to Oliver Sacks in *Seeing Voices*, the deaf who have not learned sign language live in a small world, the world of the present, the world that is concretely before their eyes. Without language, the deaf have no way to conceptualize, to step back and reflect on their choices. They are bound to the particular. Sound familiar? When noise overwhelms us, we move from one urgency to the next. We retreat into the superficial world we have decided to occupy, sometimes to such a degree that those who do not seem to care about consumer culture appear to us as odd and out of touch.

Take Jesus, for example. We are astounded that he commanded a leper not to tell anyone about being healed (Mark 1:44), and we are baffled by his silent reply to Pilate's question about where he came from (John 19:9). Although Jesus doesn't seem to understand good public relations, perhaps his choices are more consistent with divine character. First Kings 19:11-12 tells us something about the distance between God's ways and ours:

> Then a great and powerful wind tore the mountains apart and shattered the rocks before the LORD, but the LORD was not in the wind. After the wind there was an earthquake, but the LORD was not in the earthquake. After the earthquake came a fire, but the LORD was not in the fire. And after the fire came a gentle whisper.

If our church services are any measure of our desires, we seem to prefer a God of wind and earthquake and fire to a God of quiet presence. We want a showy, special-effects deity, a God at least as flashy as our culture. Otherwise, we're bored.

What the deaf lose first. When our daughters were teenagers, we sometimes argued with them about their media choices. This did not always go well. Too often we resorted to the classic stand-off: "I am wiser than you are" vs. "You are too old to possibly know what is good for me." During one of these debates, we heard this argument: "Look, seeing sex in a movie does not mean I am going to go out and hook up every night!"

Of course, literally, our daughter was right. And this got me thinking. Though we can and often do imitate blatantly depraved content in the media, perhaps we too exclusively put our focus there. Understandably, we notice what's louder and more garish. But what about the other side of the continuum, the quieter, less noticeable behaviors? Might flashy cultural vulgarities create a diversion such that we miss what is happening on the gentler side of things? Here is a simple but disregarded reality: it is easy not to hear what gets shouted down. Our larger problem may not be the gaining of imitated immoral behaviors but the losing of subtle, soft-spoken character qualities. The noise of culture overwhelms the less brassy aspects of life, including what I call *the quieter virtues:* discernment, innocence, authenticity, modesty, reverence, contentment and generosity. Because we tend not to notice these important virtues, I want to turn up their volume so we can hear what they have to tell us.

For the deaf, the sign language of virtue. If we are becoming deaf to these good things, perhaps, like the literally deaf, we need to learn a language—virtue language—a method of speaking that will help us find our way in the clutter and clamor of our existence. But there's a problem with this word *virtue.* For many of us, it doesn't just come with "baggage"; it has a hotel bellhop's rolling luggage cart packed to the top and is barely able to make it into the elevator. We see the clunky mess as the doors open, and we say, "No thanks, I'll take the stairs." To some, virtue just sounds old and stuffy, rather do-gooderish, something Greeks cared about, and Romans, and monks—all those folks who wouldn't survive our culture for a day. But virtue is, as I hope to show, relevant, necessary and exceedingly practical.

Perhaps a contemporary comparison will help. My favorite sport, tennis, provides many parallels with virtue-living. The court has boundaries. Most of the time, my goal is to smack the ball as hard as I can and keep it in the court. It isn't easy. The harder I hit the ball, the more likely it is to go out. Living a virtuous life is like this. It's living as all-out as we can while keeping our choices inside important boundaries. Sometimes we make mistakes, and the ball goes into the net or sails long or wide. So, we pick up the ball and try again. The more we focus and practice and discipline ourselves, the better things typically go.

Living as Jesus would have us live—righteously, virtuously in faith—involves not just learning from mistakes but also forgetting them, not letting them continue to beat us, haunt us or adversely influence our next shot. Being an athlete or musician or Jesus-follower is not about being perfect, and I hope you can see the virtues in this way—not as a game but as life choices that are invigorating, good for us in the way exercise is and central to all God designed us to be.

One goal of all virtue practice is greater freedom. As Paul says, "It is for freedom that Christ has set us free" (Galatians 5:1). I practice tennis so that I am free to hit the ball as I intend to hit it. Living the quieter virtues should lead to freedom, not a perfectionism consumed with moral nitpicking. For example, if I am not content, I am not free to live without what I desire. If I am not authentic, I am not free to tell a difficult truth—and so on. In the best of times, living Jesus' way of life is about the joy of playing freely.

WHAT THE QUIETER VIRTUES ARE AND AREN'T

Just as the word *virtue* has its strengths and weaknesses, so does the word *quiet*. It conjures up images of shadow-fearing wimps and shushing librarians. But the quieter virtues are as tough and bold as they need to be. One reason they are enduring is because the quieter virtues are offshoots of traditional virtues. I like to call the traditional virtues "parents" and the quieter virtues their "children." The parents are the cardinal virtues of prudence, justice, courage and temperance, and the Christian virtues of faith, hope and love. Thus, discernment is a child of prudence, innocence is a child of justice, authenticity of courage, modesty of temperance, reverence of faith, contentment of hope and generosity of love. Perhaps this familial perspective will awaken the quieter virtues more fully for you.

In addition, the quieter virtues are not necessarily quiet—and they certainly aren't timid. Though they sometimes get lost in the loudness of our culture, the quieter virtues can make a ruckus themselves. At times, authenticity (a child of courage) requires daring intensity. Reverence (a child of faith) may call for a boisterous reaction to sacrilege.

Neither are the quieter virtues dull. G. K. Chesterton reminds us that living the life of faith means giving "room for good things to run wild." We are to be fearless adventurers, not fearful tightrope walkers. If Jesus' application of the virtues ranged from controversial debates with religious leaders to dramatic prayer in the wilderness, our application need not be dull either.

One key feature in this book's treatment of each virtue is its definition. To encourage fresh thinking, I have tried to enter into these ideas from the side door, using language and perspectives that are not traditional. Along the way, dozens (even hundreds) of possible definitions have been scratched out and refined and attempted once more. I hope what remains will lead you to renewed consideration of these quieter virtues, stimulated in part by the questions supplied "for discussion or reflection" at the end of each chapter. I have at times been cryptic or suggestive rather than exhaustive. My desire is that what you read—even where it leaves you wanting more—will spark good conversation and prayer and effort.

Let us listen intently to the gentle whisper of God.

FOR DISCUSSION OR REFLECTION

1. In light of the examples in this chapter, what noise clamors for your attention?

2. To what degree has physical noise made you "breezy, shallow, unconnected"? What does this mean for your relationships?

3. Which cultural noises do you listen to the most and why: image consciousness, freedom for fun's sake, or the paradox of everythingness and nothingness?

4. What emotional voices from the past and about the future speak loudly to you?

5. Discuss 1 Kings 19:11-12. Why do you think God is sometimes loud and sometimes quiet? When do you notice the supernatural? How might you connect this discussion to the relationship between deafening noises and deafness?

6. What is your initial reaction to the idea of "quieter virtues"? If you resonate with the need for them, what attention are you giving to them?

EXERCISE

For twenty-four hours, record every exposure to the media. On an hourly basis, write down the type of media (TV, Internet, cell phone, texting, magazine, movie, all advertisements and so on) and record your response or reflection in the moment.

During the next twenty-four hours, abstain from every form of media. Do not use the phone, check e-mail, go to a movie, look at a single advertisement. Write down what you did each hour and what it was like resisting or fasting from the media.

1. What does this exercise say to you about your involvement in a noisy world? (Did you think that you "would die" during your day without media?)

2. To what degree does *addiction* or *dependence* describe your involvement with the media? What habits would you like to break, maintain or create?

2 ❧ DISCERNMENT
choosing life or cheering death

We have come to the place where I have told thee that thou shalt see the woeful people, who have lost the good of understanding.

DANTE ALIGHIERI, *INFERNO*, CANTO III

When our three daughters were young, my wife and I had an annoying habit of asking what movies were going to be shown at parties our girls attended. One time, when our two younger girls were ages seven and five, the hosting mom responded to our inquiry with, "I'm showing *Blankety-Blank*." Janet and I were absolutely dumbfounded. We had seen *Blankety-Blank* (not its real title!) several years before and knew it was not kids' fare. Not only was the lead male drunk half the time, the lead female, according to the jacket blurb, was in her "sex kitten" phase. What kind of discernment led this mom to think that this movie was a good choice?

Lest you think this example is too obvious, more nuanced stories abound. My students report struggling to distinguish between acceptable sexual content (for viewing) and pornography, truth-telling and deception, "sharing" and gossip, moderate drinking and alcohol abuse. But some of the time, they don't struggle at all. They raise two hands in worship and three beers at the bar with equal enthusiasm.

Does it seem to you that too few conversations about right and wrong choices take place these days? Concern about discernment seems to have decreased just as the need to distinguish between things—good and evil, true and false, nourishing and destructive—has grown exponentially. It is no accident that these trends have occurred at the same time.

When I speak to groups about the importance of discernment, especially as related to the media, the most common response is, "Yes, I agree—and I am so concerned for the children." An admirable sentiment. Yet I wonder, what about the adults? Are *we* immune from adverse influence? What is the state of *our* discernment? Shouldn't we be interested in developing personal character that better prepares us for wise decision making?

Making moral distinctions has never been more difficult. Compared to other eras, we have more decisions to make and more *kinds* of choices. And much of the time, there is no clear-cut right or wrong, true or false. Consider these categories:

Traditional questions:

- How "fast" should I develop my current romantic relationship?
- What do I say to a Christian friend who has been significantly immoral?
- How should I best respond to my cranky supervisor or professor?

Newer questions:

- How many hours should I play my favorite video game or talk/text on the phone or cruise the Internet or listen to music? What content is harmful for me?
- How can I live like Jesus when advertising constantly tells me what I "have to" have?

- What can be done about technological terrorism or global warming?

Although questions like these often have moral and spiritual components, the way we should interpret these components is not usually obvious. Of course, some questions of discernment are straightforward: "Should I murder my roommate tonight?" We may *feel* like doing this, but we aren't confused about what is the right choice.

Discernment matters. I love the way Annie Dillard puts it: "How we spend our days is, of course, how we spend our lives." In the moment, we might not realize the importance of making moral distinctions, but over time, the choices we make based on these distinctions work on the clay of our souls. If we ignore the shape we are taking, we might end up looking like a badly formed coffee mug instead of a sculpture that would leave Michelangelo in awe, one that beautifully represents our Father in heaven.

We forget that, without use, discernment atrophies. The writer of Hebrews recognized this: "Anyone who lives on milk, being still an infant, is not acquainted with the teaching about righteousness. But solid food is for the mature, who by constant use have trained themselves to distinguish good from evil" (5:13-14). Distinguishing between good and evil is a mark of those who are spiritually developed. It does not happen automatically. It requires training and consistent diligence—choices made difficult by three trends in our era.

THE VELVETEEN RABBIT FACTOR:
THE WEIGHT OF NOT BEING ABLE TO TELL WHAT IS REAL

In the classic children's story *The Velveteen Rabbit*, a stuffed animal bunny sits neglected in a boy's toy box, listening to more expensive toys boast as they pretend to be real. Troubled by this talk, the Rabbit turns to an older toy, the wise and experienced Skin

Horse, and asks, "What is REAL? . . . Does it mean having things that buzz inside you and a stick-out handle?" At the time, the Rabbit doesn't realize that his whole future hangs on the answer. But readers understand the point. We resonate with the story because we all yearn to be real and to know what is real—and we are delighted by the Skin Horse's answer: "When a child loves you for a long, long time, not just to play with, but REALLY loves you, then you become Real."

Yet often, in our world of technological wizardry, we cannot tell if what we see is real. Increasingly, we have absolutely no way of knowing what is natural and what is manipulated—and sometimes we are left feeling confused and unnerved. This anxiety is what I call the Velveteen Rabbit Factor, the idea that *we bear the weight of not being able to tell what is real*. We watch a movie and wonder, "Which part was digitally added?" We see an ad and ask, "What does the model actually look like?" We have a hunch that this lack of knowledge matters, that we need to know more of the truth of what we experience than we do.

Not only is it often impossible to know what is computer generated and what isn't, we don't have the time to review all the media we experience. It comes at us too quickly. If we are confronted with thousands of ads a day, as researchers report, how can we hope to sort them out? And ads are just the tip of the media-berg. There's e-mail and the Internet and movies and music, ad infinitum.

Understanding what is real has become so difficult that much of the time we don't ask or care. In *Mediated*, Thomas de Zengotita says, "The issue isn't *can* we [make these distinctions]; it's *do* we do it—and the answer is, of course not. How could we?" If we can't know whether something is genuine or counterfeit, historical or invented, true or false, what problems does this deficiency create?

I'm not sure that the lack of knowledge itself harms us, but I am convinced that the Velveteen Rabbit Factor reinforces our natural laziness toward the work of making distinctions. We abdicate our responsibility to discern, resulting in occasional conversations such as this:

Chris: "What'd you think of the movie last night?"

Pat: "It was good."

Chris: "What about it was good?"

Pat: "Huh? I just felt it was entertaining."

Chris: "Hmm. What about the way the good guy cheated on his friends?"

Pat: "Whatever."

Chris's line of questions may not be typical, but Pat's answers are. Because we are overwhelmed with so many difficult discernments, we retreat into "I feel" and "whatever," reducing our responses to emotions and non-assertions so that they won't be challenged. Sometimes we opt out of making moral distinctions because we've grown accustomed to opting out of "reality" distinctions. If it doesn't matter if I can discern the degrees of deception in special effects, do the finer points of deception in my own speech really matter?

But this abdicating leap is unnecessary. Although the Velveteen Rabbit Factor may leave us burdened and confused, good discernment does not depend on the ability to put every form of reality accurately into neat boxes. C. S. Lewis understood this years before our more mediated age: "In fact we should never ask of anything 'Is it real?' for everything is real. The proper question is, 'A real *what*?'" Movies are real. Websites are real. Even fantasies are real; they are real acts of imagination. Instead of examining the degree of natural reality in each cinematic scene, we might examine ourselves to see if we have given up on the virtue of discernment.

CHOOSAK: THE APPEARANCE OF
MAKING IMPORTANT CHOICES

Without elevators or supermarkets, we might never have had Musak, the programming that takes rough edges off popular songs and spins them out in blobby blandness. Without Malcolm Muggeridge, we might never have had the term "newsak," his way of describing the incessant stream of chatty news that greets us everywhere. And without the proliferation of options, we might never have had "choosak," my term that describes the appearance of making important choices, when, for the most part, we are making insignificant decisions, such as which microwave meal to eat, whether we should buy another T-shirt or what is the shortest route between one errand and the next.

The main problem with choosak is that it fools us into thinking we are doing the good work of discernment. If we agonize over decisions, doesn't that mean we are actively discerning? In some sense, yes—but we often agonize over such trivial things. We congratulate ourselves for reaching a myriad of mundane conclusions, even as we ignore more meaningful issues such as poverty in our city or neighbors whose marriage is in shambles or friends who want to talk with us about a deeper faith.

Choosak plays into (or perhaps derives from) the American love of efficiency. One supervisor of mine required all employees to chart what we did every fifteen minutes for several days. Afterward, we were pressured to discern how we could be more efficient with our time. But how would we know we were more efficient? Greater productivity, of course. And how would we know we were being productive? Quantitative results, of course. Ultimately, as we spent hours justifying what we already knew to be effective, we were wasting the very time we were supposed to be saving. Choosak! Choosak! Everything is choosak!

The number of mundane choices can also paralyze us. Years ago, when we moved into our current house, we had to make dozens of decisions in a short period. I remember staring with exasperation at fifteen swatches of beige carpet. I shouted to my decision-reluctant wife, "I don't care! Just pick one!" We may be exhausted (and grumpy) from sorting out the options, but that does not mean we have developed discernment well. In fact, choosak has a way of sanitizing discernment in the same way that Musak sanitizes music. All decisions, momentous or not, begin to feel the same.

THE IMAGINARIUM: WE BELIEVE WE GAIN EXPERIENCE WITHOUT EFFECT

I love images. I love visual beauty. I love the places novels and movies take me. By the Imaginarium, I am not referring to the fundamental qualities of our imagination—nor am I referring to an aisle in a toy store. Contending with the Imaginarium is a way of saying that, increasingly, living in an image-saturated culture leads us to think that, as spectators, we can gain experience without being affected by that experience.

After a hard day of work, we look forward to downtime. For many of us, this means time in front of a screen or, as we often put it, "vegging out." Hours thus logged have led us to become remarkably skilled as spectators. Sometimes we watch and learn or critique, but often we merely watch. We tend to "take things in" without thinking, coping with the overload of images with a numbing passivity.

In his book *Touch*, Gabriel Josipovici says, "Sight is free and sight is irresponsible." What he means is that looking at something—a mountain peak, for example—requires little physical or moral effort. Hiking to the peak is altogether different. There's nothing wrong with seeing as such, or using a camera, but our watching can become obsessive and can skew our way of perceiving. When it does, we view too much of life as just more stuff on the screen, as material to look at but kept at arm's length. We say we've *experi-*

enced something when we have only watched it. We "travel the world" but never leave our living room. Watching passively encourages uncritical acceptance and discourages discernment.

We also cope with the Imaginarium by becoming "ock jocks," my shorthand for "ocular tough guys" (that helps, huh?). Ock jocks are viewers who brag they can watch anything—the Internet, computer games, TV, movies—and not be adversely influenced. They say they are thick skinned, impervious to whatever graphic violence or sex or twisted values they see.

Ock jocks think they can completely control how they are affected by images. But can anyone truly absorb every thought, every image, and remain unscathed? Isn't that why we engage with any media in the first place, to be *affected* by it—to relieve our boredom or hear a comforting sentiment? At the very least, aren't these effects? And how can we possibly be so skilled as to resist the influence of all intended messages? Isn't this more than any human could hope to achieve? Though I teach media literacy, I can still get caught up in an image of a digitally manipulated supermodel. Analysis doesn't keep me from saying, "Wow, that face is beautiful."

I also wonder, What is so admirable about achieving a state of being unchanged by what we encounter? When we harden our exterior to the messages around us, we lose sensitivity to the things that ought to move us. If our goal is to be untouched, we won't "rejoice with those who rejoice; mourn with those who mourn" (Romans 12:15). Because a pastor in Belize did not want to become indifferent to tragedy, he made a choice. He said, "I don't watch the news. The stories move so quickly that I don't have time to grieve." This admission stuns us, because we watch the news—and are rarely moved. But perhaps we are being moved toward desensitization.

Ock jocks dare the media world to do its worst, to come at them with both barrels. *We're tough,* they tell themselves. *We can take it.*

Curiously, when they find themselves all shot up (with pride or lust or anger), they tend not to see any connection to their choices. The Imaginarium can leave us passive and hardened.

What are the results of contending with these three forces? The worst consequence is that Christians, as Ken Myers puts it, "have thus succeeded in being of the world, but not in the world." With impoverished discernment, we turn wisdom and foolishness upside-down. Messages of crude stupidity and vigilante justice are praised while humility and faith are ridiculed. We accept the "wink, wink" world of Las Vegas, a location famous for keeping confidences about immoral choices. Yet Isaiah 5:20 says, "Woe to those who call evil good and good evil, who put darkness for light and light for darkness, who put bitter for sweet and sweet for bitter."

Our secularization is in part, I believe, due to the neglect of the virtue of discernment; it isn't in the "constant use" Hebrews recommends. The Velveteen Rabbit Factor, the weight of not being able to tell what is real, can lead us to forsake the work of discernment. Choosak, the many trivial decisions that give us a false sense of wise decision making, can paralyze our commitment to discernment. And the Imaginarium, the seductions of an image-saturated culture, can numb and harden us to the analysis required for discernment. What can we do to offset these trends? If we are sick, we may need to see a doctor.

BECOMING A GOOD PHYSIOGNOMIST

In *The Man Who Mistook His Wife for a Hat*, neurologist Oliver Sacks reviews the case of a patient whose eyes appeared to work well, but his brain couldn't correctly categorize what he saw. He thought a glove was a clever invention for storing coins, and when he left Sacks's office, he reached for his wife's face as if it were a hat. Funny—in a macabre way—but also immensely tragic.

Discernment is all about physiognomy, as a medical dictionary puts it: "the art of discovering temperament and character from outward appearance." Having good physiognomy means recognizing the true character of what we are seeing. I find this idea fascinating. We may physically see something "accurately" but not see it for what it really is. This faculty applies to gloves and faces, but it also goes for movies and marriage and motivational talks.

Discernment is the prudence to practice moral physiognomy; it is the ability to draw accurate conclusions about what is before us. Just as "the man who mistook his wife for a hat" had difficulty negotiating his way through life, so a person void of moral physiognomy would make foolish choices. But imagine a person highly skilled in moral physiognomy, a kind of superhero with "discernment vision" who could immediately tell whether a choice was wise or not. Although we might not become superheroes, all of us can develop this kind of vision. Sacks puts it this way: "Judgment is the most important faculty we have. An animal, or a man, may get on very well without 'abstract attitude' but will speedily perish if deprived of judgment." Sizing things up, making judgments, practicing discernment is at the heart of who we are and who we are becoming. As we develop discernment, we are imitating God, who is the Great Physiognomist. He knows our hearts. Through our outward appearance, he sees our true character—and he is looking for life.

CHOOSING LIFE OR DEATH

During my first visit to the United States Holocaust Memorial Museum in Washington, D.C., after plodding through the horrors of the extermination of the Jews by the Nazis, after seeing familiar but always disturbing photos of emaciated bodies, after seeing a whole room filled with shoes taken from prisoners about to get gassed, I entered one last space, a sanctuary set aside for contemplation. There, inscribed in stone in the center, was a version of Deuteronomy 30:19: "This day I call heaven and earth as witnesses against you that I have set before you life and death, blessings and curses. Now choose life, so that you and your children may live." Questions raced in and through me:

What does it mean to choose life instead of death?

How could human beings have chosen such brutality?

Why did some people risk their lives to assist the weak?

What holocausts are looming in our times?

As important as these questions are, I want to focus on how they reveal certain assumptions about the life-and-death nature of our decisions. The more I thought about choosing life and choosing death, the more I realized that choosing life in the little things prepares us for choosing life in tougher, more monumental situations. And I saw that these choices are at the heart of discernment.

At first glance, life-and-death choices seem to pertain primarily to clear-cut options: A child is drowning in rough surf. Do I swim out to save her? A man points a gun into a crowd. Do I call 911? Only a sociopath or a coward would say no—but these kinds of examples miss the great insight of the larger Deuteronomy passage: life-and-death decisions are not limited to extreme circumstances:

> Now what I am commanding you today is not too difficult for you or beyond your reach. . . . See, I set before you today life and prosperity, death and destruction. . . . I have set before you life and death, blessings and curses. Now choose life, so that you and your children may live and that you may love the LORD your God, listen to his voice, and hold fast to him. (30:11, 15, 19-20)

To be sure, life and prosperity are set against death and destruction. But life choices are also described as loving God and walking in obedience to him. Death choices involve turning our hearts away, being disobedient and worshiping other gods. As we put on a deuteronomic lens, we begin to see how choices between life and death confront us all day long, not just when physical life is at risk.

These choices between life and death yield tangible consequences. Choose life and live; choose death and die. Sounds simple enough. The problem is that choosing life is set up as obeying all of God's rules, something we know we can't do. Are the decisions between life and death cosmic tricks? All you have to do is choose life to live—but "ha, ha, ha, you can't do it"?

Deuteronomy 30:11 addresses this question: "what I am commanding you today is not too difficult for you or beyond your reach." Choosing life is not so obscure that we need a mystical map and a knight's courage. "No, the word is very near you; it is in your mouth and in your heart so you may obey it" (v. 14). This is good news.

Even so, we have choices to make. This passage teaches that discernment is absolutely crucial for living well and that it is something we know well enough to pursue. In light of this passage in Deuteronomy, I define discernment as *the wisdom to recognize the difference between life and death—with the motivation to choose life.*

Discernment is a child of prudence, or wisdom. Before we make the outer choice that might reveal our wisdom, we make an inner choice about what is "of life" and what is "of death." These distinctions help us see what Jesus meant when he said, "I am the way and the truth and the life" (John 14:6) and "I have come that they may have life, and have it to the full" (John 10:10). Also, the book of Proverbs asserts that the person learning wisdom is engaged in the best education possible and is able to avoid being foolish. A typical verse is "The wisdom of the prudent is to give thought to their ways, but the folly of fools is deception" (14:8). Learning to be wise necessarily entails learning to make better judgments.

FRAMING CHOICES AS "LIFE AND DEATH"

How long would you survive on your own in the wilderness? Some of you would say, "About ten minutes." Others of you have specialized knowledge that would keep you alive for weeks. Among other things, you would need to know what to eat. As told in the film version of *Into the Wild*, adventurer Christopher McCandless lived alone for months in Alaska's mountains. He survived until he misinterpreted the seeds of a poisonous plant—and he died for this one mistake.

What is true for physical health is also true for moral and spiritual health. "Reading the signs" is important. We can misread relational poison (sexual temptation) and suffer relational death (adultery and divorce). We can ignore what we know about fictional fatty foods (stories that say we should always believe in ourselves) and, over a long period, increase the likelihood of narrative-inspired cardiac arrest (self-deceived arrogance). Those interested in discernment must look for all kinds of poison, for as Tim Challis points out, "We cannot affirm the existence of truth without also affirming the existence of error."

From "life" to "life nurturing." Biology teaches that natural environments are vigorous when *life-sustaining* choices are made and when *life-threatening* circumstances are addressed. When I visited Everglades National Park, the ranger held up an apple snail shell and said the Army Corp of Engineers did not take seriously the way their work draining the swamp would kill so many apple snails and lead to a massive decrease in the bird population. We need to attend to what is life sustaining and life threatening.

These categories, part of what the fields of counseling and communication studies call Systems Theory, can help us grasp the everyday practicality of viewing our circumstances as life-and-death choices. For example, a Christian couple I know divorced after twenty-five years of marriage. Toward the end, Alice blamed Tom for things he did during their first few years of marriage, things about which she had never confronted him. Tom made his share of mistakes in the relationship, but Alice's silence all those years hurt the "system" of their marriage because she chose not to address what she saw as Tom's life-threatening behaviors. By the time she voiced the issues, she had already made up her mind that the marriage was over.

In light of Systems Theory, the virtue of discernment keeps two questions before us: What is life nurturing? What is death nurturing? As a way to understand these questions, consider Paul's specifics in Galatians: Death could be seen as "sexual immorality, impurity and debauchery; idolatry and witchcraft; hatred, discord, jealousy, fits of rage, selfish ambition, dissensions, factions and envy; drunkenness, orgies, and the like" (5:19-21). Life could be seen as "love, joy, peace, patience, kindness, goodness, faithfulness, gentleness and self-control" (5:22-23). As much as these categories add concrete detail, they don't make discernment black and white.

Life and death in percentages. What makes discernment difficult is all the nasty gray. Some thoroughly awful conversations leave us feeling slimed or disillusioned; some terrific ones leave us feeling inspired and grateful. But most of our experiences do not neatly divide into 100-percent life nurturing (a story about a discouraged teacher who learns she is beloved by God) and 100-percent death affirming (a story that praises the murdering of small children as they walk to school). Instead, we engage in a kind of subliminal moral calculation, computing if the percentage of life in some event is greater than the percentage of death.

We are all familiar with these calculations. Some of our friends are smug and spiteful but also shrewd and insightful. Some websites we frequently visit "name" certain truths about political life, but their humor is vulgar and full of ridicule. On the other hand, sometimes we watch TV for light entertainment—and that is all that we get. In all of the above, discernment involves disciplining ourselves toward more life-nurturing choices.

In particular, life-and-death calculations inform our responses to the three trends I mentioned earlier in the chapter. Concerning the Velveteen Rabbit Factor, the question is not "what is real?" but "what, in this event, gives life?" Concerning Choosak, the question is not "am I prepared to make choices?" but "am I prepared to make life-affirming choices?" Concerning the Imaginarium, the question is not "am I tough enough to handle these images?" but "which images, on the whole, move me more toward life or more toward death?" We do our best to follow Jesus with these questions, to sort out the will of God when it seems uncertain.

Is God's will murky? It depends on the topic at hand. We know God's precise will about the most important things: our salvation, our commitment to loving God and our neighbor. Even so, huge discernments remain: "Should I marry this person I'm dating? Should I take the job across the country? What can I do about my friend's depression?" You know the kind of issues I'm talking about.

While my idea of discernment certainly doesn't resolve all questions about God's will, it gets us asking good questions. During a tense committee meeting, a colleague of mine said, "I'm not exactly sure what God's will is regarding this personnel decision, but I do know that God wills for us to act lovingly along the way." On the precipice of any difficult discussion, we could ask, "Am I choosing life or am I choosing death?" If we possess a "choosing life" lens, are we more likely to make the wiser choice? Yes, I think so, but another refinement to this lens will help us sort things out.

FOUR LIFE-AND-DEATH OPTIONS

Sometimes, commencement presents difficult and awkward circumstances for my students. A week before graduation, Kristen asked me, "How am I supposed to cope with seeing my newly divorced parents? How should I act toward Dad's new girlfriend, the one he left Mom for, the one who is only five years older than I am? What should I say when Mom blasts Dad?"

In situations like these, we recognize that there are different ways to prepare for choosing life. How important is our inner attitude, the heart motive that Jesus emphasizes in the Sermon on the Mount when he says that anger and lust are part of murder and adultery? Certainly, we can choose life outwardly but not mean it. Paul addressed this issue in Romans 12:9: "Love must be sincere. Hate what is evil; cling to what is good." We can choose life insincerely. We can make a loving choice but feel bitter on the inside. Because of these alternatives, I believe we can pursue life and death in four different ways. These ways could be seen as steps we move through, but more likely, they are separate options we could pick.

We can choose death and love it. The worst choice we can make is to enjoy the evil we engage in. You might think this category is reserved for mass murderers and other flagrant criminals. Not so. Kristen might look forward to slandering her dad. Any of us can revel in revenge or savor our lust. A key part of discernment is being willing to admit that these enjoyments are forms of death.

We can choose death and hate it. A better but still destructive choice is to do evil while stating truth to ourselves about our choice. Kristen might engage in gossip, then catch herself and wish she had not done so. Although the damage of her harsh comments might continue moving in her circle of friends, she has named her decision accurately. She has discerned death as death. Sometimes this category leads to guilt mongering toward ourselves and others—but it can also lead to new attitudes and actions. Paul himself says, "What a wretched man I am! Who will rescue me from this body of death?" (Romans 7:24).

We can choose life and hate it. Unfortunately, all of us are skilled at smiley hypocrisy. Kristen might decide she should "be nice" to her dad and his girlfriend, all the while wishing she could really let loose and let him have it. If so, her desire is toward death. We might graciously offer help to a guy whose car battery is dead but curse him for making us late for a meeting. Though these choices are socially superior (I am glad that those who are angry with me do not actually hit me), they are, in some ways, spiritually inferior. When choosing death and hating it, we are at least telling the truth. When choosing life and hating it, we are living a lie. Our motive matters.

We can choose life and love it. The best option of all is to enjoy doing the good, "to *love* mercy," as Micah 6:8 puts it (italics mine). As Kristen discerns what to do, she might conclude that the most life-nurturing choice would be to forgive her father without forsaking the importance of speaking the truth in love. I don't want this choice to sound sentimental, as if it were easy. But I do want us to see that the highest good involves giving ourselves wholeheartedly to life. How much better it is when we *enjoy* washing a friend's car or giving money to someone in need. The best discernment includes the heart.

Having the prudence to recognize the difference between life and death—and to choose life—is not the path of a knee-jerk reactionary. It is thoughtful work. It requires a commitment to nuance and good question-asking. In addition, as with all of the quieter virtues, discernment is aided by a spiritual discipline, a "practice" that puts us in a better position to follow through. Since I will present a corresponding spiritual discipline for each of the quieter virtues, I thought I should in this first chapter put in a good word for this kind of training.

Spiritual disciplines prepare our minds and hearts for obedience, like all rehearsal. Musicians train so that when their key moment arrives, they will perform as they desire. Sometimes we think that because salvation is a gift, work of any kind should not be involved in spiritual maturity. Yet receiving a gift does not mean we need not work to accentuate it, any more than a world-class sprinter would expect to win the Olympic 100 meters without practice. In all things, we sincerely hope and pray for God's grace, but Paul also tells us to "work out your salvation with fear and trembling" (Philippians 2:12).

Often practice means rehearsing the same thing we are going to later perform, but sometimes practice involves exercises that don't exactly mimic what we are preparing to do. Even though football rarely looks like ballet, football players engage in dance-like foot drills. Likewise, novelists might play word games, the results of which will never directly find their way into a story. The disciplines I suggest are of this sort: ways to train for the virtue but not in the practice-the-exact-piano-piece-for-the-recital sense. They are more like the foundation for the house we are attempting to build, essential structure but not always seen. I hope you catch the vision for these disciplines.

✥ THE DISCIPLINE OF ATTENTIVENESS

Sometimes I think our whole culture has Restless Fly Disorder. We buzz around constantly, and we can't seem to land anywhere for long. With all the available diversions, we flit. We can't stay on task. Or maybe we act more like an air-hockey puck, bouncing noisily off the walls. Bing, bing, BING! We are on the move. "Focus" is a byword for our times.

A counterpoint to this scattershot behavior is the discipline of *attentiveness,* which can be seen as *the stewardship of the present.* We can miss the present in so many ways. We can live in regrets of the past. We can live in fear of the future. We can suffer the grass-is-greener syndrome, jerking our heads here and there like birds on the lookout for the next crumb.

Attentiveness means that we have a sense of responsibility to notice what is happening in the moment, what the moment calls for and what the moment is calling out of us. As Henry James said to prospective writers, "Try to be one of the people on whom nothing is lost." Without becoming obsessive, we can listen well and respond appropriately. How can we learn to be more attentive?

In the garden of attentiveness, eradicate and cultivate. Two years into our marriage, my wife and I bought our first home, an older, neglected, tiny place near the railroad tracks. We were thrilled. I couldn't wait to prepare soil in the backyard for a vegetable garden. The problem was that the entire area was covered in devil-grass roots so thick that I had to roll them up like a rug. The former owner also had a crazy habit of scattering stuff he salvaged from the train yard. I pulled out gears and license plates and small tables. And then there was the rotten wood filled with disgusting termites.

A simple truth directed my work: Before I could plant the

seeds, I had to get everything out that didn't belong; I had to *eradicate*. Then I could *cultivate*. I turned the soil, planted, watered, fertilized and kept pests away. I gave my energy to maintain the garden. ·

To be attentive stewards of the present, we must learn to eradicate—to block out, to fence off, to say no to everything except the object of our attentions. So much of the time, we go through the motions of our daily tasks mindlessly, habitually, unreflectively. We need to become not multitaskers but uni-taskers, resisting the popular thought that the more we can cram into a moment, the more we achieve. "I don't understand why I can't concentrate enough to read," we say. "I put the TV on low, take out one of my earbuds and only answer every other text message." Instead of loading up every second, attentiveness requires an emptying of all but one thing. It requires mindfulness.

We must also learn to cultivate—to gather in, to coax toward us, to say yes to everything that is related to the object of our attention. With better concentration, we might attend to a friend's story so closely we could repeat it in fine detail. We might pray, thinking only about God's goodness, grace and patience.

A friend of mine reads the Gospels straight through once a year, asking a different question each time. One year he asked, "How does Jesus practice grace?" Another year, "What does Jesus say about money?" This single-mindedness is a way of being attentive to Jesus.

It's not easy to focus well. Since, in an information age, as Richard Lanham argues, "attention is the commodity in short supply," we are constantly being persuaded to look here and look there, to notice clever design and attractive presentation. We are encouraged to flit reactively. As good stewards of the present, we get closer to Paul's idea that we should "not be mastered by anything" (1 Corinthians 6:12), and we see life and death more clearly. Our discernment improves.

When eradication includes stepping away from common involvements—what we traditionally call fasting or abstinence—we discover that "doing without" actually gives us more. Avoid shopping malls for a few months, and you might be shocked by the garish consumerism when you return. Refrain from cynical acquaintances for a time, and you might notice destructive talk when you reenter their world.

When cultivation develops single-mindedness, we may observe certain good things more frequently: the loving actions of a cashier or the generous enthusiasm of a teenager. A painting, a psychological theory or a software program might seem rich with the image of God. As we practice the stewardship of the present, we learn to love what God loves, to notice life as the real thing it is, to choose life with all our hearts.

Most of us gravitate toward the phrase "lifelong learner." The quieter virtue of discernment informs the idea. As we seek the wisdom to recognize the difference between life and death—with the motivation to choose life—we commit ourselves to be *life*long learners, to be *life*-wide and *life*-deep learners. Thus we may say with Paul, "Finally, brothers and sisters, whatever is true, whatever is noble, whatever is right, whatever is pure, whatever is lovely, whatever is admirable—if anything is excellent or praiseworthy—think about such things" (Philippians 4:8).

FOR DISCUSSION AND REFLECTION

1. Consider Philippians 1:9-10: "And this is my prayer: that your love may abound more and more in knowledge and depth of insight, so that you may be able to discern what is best and may be pure and blameless for the day of Christ." On a scale of one (poor) to five (excellent), how would you rate yourself overall as a discerner? Why?

2. Explain how the three cultural trends affect your discernment:

    a. The Velveteen Rabbit Factor: When do you feel the burden of not being able to tell what is real?

    b. Choosak: What important decisions do you neglect because you are busy with less significant ones?

    c. The Imaginarium: How would you characterize your relationship to our image-saturated culture? To what degree are you an ock jock?

3. Provide some examples of good physiognomy, especially when the true, moral character of the object is revealed to be other than what it appears. Consider a film, a popular saying or a time when a friend "saw through you" to your real condition.

4. When you think about the definition of discernment, "the wisdom to recognize the difference between life and death—with the motivation to choose life," what sorts of things are informed by putting things in life-or-death terms? What situations don't seem to be able to be reduced to these terms?

5. What do you think of the idea of "life and death in percentages"? Does this perspective dilute strong responses to what is right and wrong?

6. List personal examples for each of the "four life-and-death options." Ask a close friend to look at your list, or discuss it with your small group. In what ways do your friends agree or not agree with your examples? What life-giving choice would you like to enjoy more fully, instead of merely being dutiful?

EXERCISE

Go someplace busy, such as a city street or a coffee shop. Practice attentiveness by concentrating on one thing to the exclusion of all distractions. For example, see how long you can read without being diverted, or see how long you can pray without drifting mindlessly. Attempt to concentrate again, this time doubling the length of time from your first try. Record what you needed to eradicate (abstain from) and what you needed to cultivate (mindfully focus on). Now go someplace very quiet and do the same. Which situation is more difficult for you?

3 ❧ INNOCENCE
lost and found

(We have) by innocence cast out anchors for our souls to keep them from shipwreck, though they be not kept from storm.

JEREMY TAYLOR

During one of my Grand-tours-of-Europe-on-a-less-than-grand-budget, I began in Rome and traveled north. By the time I stepped into Munich's Alte Pinakothek art gallery, I had seen dozens of glorious buildings and hundreds of historic paintings. Many of the latter were images of Jesus crucified, the Madonna and Child, and the arrow-pierced gore of St. Sebastian. I tried to appreciate each one, but the monotony was enough to make me want to forsake any gold-flecked thing for a good long while.

As I rounded a corner, I saw Rubens's *Massacre of the Innocents*, a wreck of violence and agony. Though often forgotten in the sentimentality heaped on the Christmas season, Herod's decision to murder every male child in Bethlehem under two years of age can still elicit gasps of disbelief. After the Magi failed to provide undercover intelligence about the Messiah, Herod multiplied every parent's nightmare a thousandfold by sending his troops in the night to kill these defenseless boys (Matthew 2:1-18).

In that moment in the gallery, the painting pierced me like one of St. Sebastian's arrows. I pictured myself as one of the fathers, delirious with grief and anger, wailing before Herod and God and anyone who might listen. When innocents are slaughtered, we stumble and weep. Our sense of injustice cries out, sometimes till it grows hoarse. If our own innocent child is taken, the tragedy is unspeakable.

Reflecting on this painting one day, I made a mental jump from *innocents* to *innocence*. Might the massacre of innocents have some insight for us, for our era's abuse of power against what is good and true and beautiful? In particular, is one of the chief power brokers of our times, Hollywood, slaughtering our innocence?

HEROD'S MOTIVES AND HOLLYWOOD'S METHODS

To make such a brutal decision, Herod's fear of competition must have been monstrous. He must have been panicked about the future influence of an innocent child, one who might later lead a revolt. So, following the parallel, I ask, does Hollywood fear the power of innocence?

Take a recent romance-competition TV show,* one that aired before dinner, when children could easily tune in. A man attempted to narrow his dating choices from three women to one by asking an important compatibility question. Of course, he asked her opinion on friendship or foreign policy, right? No. He asked, "What is your favorite sexual position?" After one embarrassed woman opted out of the rivalry (clearly the loser), the "chosen one" specified a position. Without a hint of shame, the man then asked, "Will you show me right now?" Equally unrestrained, she did, using available furniture as her partner.

---

*So that I don't needlessly make this book out-of-date, I will avoid specific titles where I can. As I refer to a genre, you can imagine some current TV show or movie. There are plenty of examples to choose from.

Like Herod, Hollywood appears to gain from this kind of attack on innocence. The entertainment industry would prefer that audiences not ask potentially restricting questions such as, "Will the content of this show damage something good in me?" To Hollywood, innocence is a financial threat because uncorrupted audiences are less likely to be seduced by the temptations designed into most media advertising campaigns. Hollywood—not monolithically or conspiratorially but on the whole—seeks to maintain power at the expense of thoughtful moral consistency.

So if there are any reasonable parallels between Herod and Hollywood, if innocence is in some sense being demeaned, defiled, trampled, even massacred, one searing issue presents itself: Where is the weeping and wailing in our times? Where are the mothers and fathers mourning the loss of innocence? Perhaps we are not mourning because, by and large, we have given up our sons and daughters without resistance. We invite Herod right into our homes with all his weapons drawn.

A FEW INNOCENT QUESTIONS

Before I say more about the nature of innocence, I would like to offer some questions for your consideration.

- *Are you innocent?* (Is innocence restricted to children? If not, how might adult innocence differ from childhood innocence?)

- *Can a person become innocent?* (Is it a quality that can be practiced, or is it a state that, once violated, is forever corrupted?)

- *How might you be better off if you were more innocent?* (What do your answers to this question say about the nature of innocence?)

- *What is the mass media's relationship to your innocence?* (When does media content attack your innocence, and when does the content inspire it?)

- *When innocence is lost, what is lost?* (Does "lost innocence" refer only to the fact of a broken boundary, or can you identify particular losses?)

As you compose your answers, try to keep guilt from dominating. We have *all* wounded our innocence to varying degrees; that's one reason we are drawn to God's love. Instead, put your efforts toward understanding the quality of innocence itself. In what sense might it be a virtue?

THE NATURE OF INNOCENCE

Of all the character qualities suggested in this book, innocence is the least intuitive. Contrary to our typical use of the term, when I talk about innocence as a virtue, I am thinking of it as a *decision* we make. This is why John Izzo calls it "second innocence, . . . a choice to reclaim our trust and faith in the world." The virtue of innocence is not the same thing as a state of inexperience into which we were born.

Since the parent virtue of innocence is justice, innocence is informed by the metaphor of a jury trial. In the courtroom, we learn if those accused have made choices that confirm innocence or guilt. If they are innocent and are acquitted, they are free. If they are guilty, they suffer consequences. So, as a virtue, innocence is related to maintaining "permissible" behaviors that lead to freedom and staying away from "criminal" ones that imprison us. G. K. Chesterton makes a similar connection between innocence and justice, but with a developmental twist: "Children are innocent and love justice while most of us are wicked and naturally prefer mercy." Maybe this is why innocence is not intuitive to adults.

In its Latin roots, *innocence* is drawn from *in* (without) *nocere* (harm or wickedness). It means "not causing harm," as in "not guilty of crimes" or "not being wicked or doing wicked things." Although none of us is perfect, one of the New Testament words for innocence, *adolos* (see 1 Peter 2:2), refers to ordinary people whose purity helps them resist deception. So innocence can be seen as related to both an inexperienced state we are born into and a quality of life we choose.

Innocence as something we, *for the most part*, outgrow. In our culture, we usually see innocence as a state of ignorance that should eventually be put aside. We apply it almost exclusively to children. Though we may disagree about the timing, we parents protect our children from certain kinds of knowledge until they are ready to acquire the information.

When I was watching a football game one day, a commercial came on for a sleazy mini-series. A woman in lingerie walked saucily toward the camera, then kissed a man in open-mouthed passion. I did not know that one of my daughters, age six at the time, was watching the scene from behind me. She said, "Daddy, why are they kissing like *this?*" and then she proceeded to imitate the woman. I smiled at her silly face—and then I grew sad. I knew that someday I would need to explain various stages of intimacy to her, but I had hoped to wait until she was older. Innocence can be seen as a kind of ignorance that gradually passes away as part of normal social development.

Innocence as something we shouldn't outgrow. Most of the time, we are hard pressed to think of good reasons to be ignorant. And why should we? Education is a terrific thing. But innocence is related to a *good* kind of ignorance, ignorance of information or behavior that corrupts. As all therapists know, certain types of exposure or experience can taint a person and contribute to dysfunction and immorality.

Consider one of my students. At age four, Kelly saw her father hitting her mother. Her father, recognizing the transgression to Kelly's innocence, said, "Don't worry, Kelly. This is what married people do who love each other." He wrapped his arms around her and attempted to comfort her. Kelly, now in her twenties, says,

"From this experience, I learned how to lie—and did so on a daily basis well into adolescence." A good case could be made that Kelly's lying would have been far less acceptable to her had she not experienced this innocence-breaking event at such a young age.

In part, innocence has to do with how we maintain this ignorance about evil. Some forms of innocence are not meant to be "passed through." Roger Shattuck says,

> What has happened to the venerable notion of forbidden knowledge? In the practicalities of daily living, we accept constraints ranging from environmental regulations to traffic lights. In matters of the mind and its representations, Western thinkers and institutions increasingly reject limits of any kind as unfounded and stultifying.

Doesn't some information harm us, regardless of age? Perhaps this is why Jesus told his adult disciples to "be as shrewd as snakes and as innocent as doves" (Matthew 10:16). He combined the purity and peacefulness of doves with the wariness and quick-strike capabilities of snakes.

Innocence is not *mere* ignorance. Without shrewdness, innocence is naiveté; shrewdness without innocence is cynicism. Paul issues a similar command: "Be wise about what is good, and innocent about what is evil" (Romans 16:19). Innocence is both a state to be outgrown and a virtue to be maintained.

INNOCENCE DEFINED

As both a condition and a choice, innocence is *our sense of justice that sets good things free and binds up evil.* As a child of justice, innocence affirms the "not guilty" in all that is good. It celebrates the good with appreciative wonder and joy, and attempts to liberate goodness when it might otherwise be restrained. At the same time, innocence understands how "guilty" evil really is. It is not uninformed. In fact, innocence denounces evil's crimes and establishes boundaries that attempt to keep evil from having its way. And insofar as it is able, innocence accomplishes all this without experiencing evil firsthand. Innocence desires and gladly partici- pates in the good, while it responds to its knowledge of evil by doing what must be done to avoid evil choices.

What does innocence look like? It might take the shape of someone who, despite difficult circumstances, does not lose heart. When my daughter Hannah was in college, she befriended an epi- leptic girl of eighteen. Because of almost daily seizures, Sarah had the maturity level of a twelve-year-old. Despite Sarah's disabilities, Hannah greeted Sarah with a warmth and joy that had been liber- ated from worrying about how others might perceive her. Yet Han- nah is not ignorant of evil. She saw moral problems in Sarah's home and knew firsthand how governmental bureaucracy could affect the assistance that Sarah did and did not receive. At times she struggles with cynicism or lack of hope, yet she models inno- cence well.

Innocence and goodness. On my first sabbatical, Janet and I drove our three girls across the country in February, from still- leafy California to bare-branched Virginia. When March and April rolled around, we experienced our first dramatic bursting forth of spring. Seeing redbuds blooming and hillsides of green exploding with color, we couldn't help but laugh out loud. We twirled around without shame, smiling and whooping it up.

Innocence is like this. It sets the good free with the childlike joy of a toddler picking up every rock and enjoying the colors and sparkles, but—here is the important difference—it does this as an adult, fully aware that rocks can be used as weapons. When we practice innocence, we say yes to every good impulse and idea. We live in the liberty of God's delight. As Paul put it, "It is for freedom that Christ has set us free" (Galatians 5:1).

When innocence liberates our best impulses, we are free to "do what love asks us to do." Sometimes fear or pride holds us back, but innocence moves us to do the good thing, to give someone a hug or a compliment, or invite someone over, or express gratitude, or help out a poorer person, or take a creative risk, or bring Jesus into a conversation. Before missionary Hudson Taylor left for his work in China, he spent Sunday afternoons wandering around the grimmer areas of London. By setting his time free from a set agenda, he could meet needs as he saw them.

Innocence and evil. Innocence binds up evil, a task sometimes as simple as saying no. At other times, restricting evil is as complex as constructing a network of counter-intelligence. One problem with evil, as we know, is that it is both "out there," in the workplace, at school, in the leisure industry, and "in here," inside our minds and hearts.

To bind evil is to restrict it, to set a barrier against it. One image is of a prison, with evil represented as a crazed criminal behind bars, shackled to the wall, starving from lack of food. It's a workable image. Of some evils—murder, torture or rape, for example—we are absolutely intolerant.

Another image is of painting evil into a corner and then painting the corner. At some point, certain vices seem not to exist for us anymore. One day, shopping in a drug store as a young boy, I slipped a candy bar into my pocket. A clerk caught me and said, "What do you think you are doing?" Sheepishly, I pulled it out and said, "I was just trying to see if it fit into my pocket." Though I can still be a smart-aleck today, stealing is no longer a temptation for me—as I suspect it is not for you. Some moral choices get painted into a corner and cease to trouble us. That's when we are truly free.

A third image of restricting evil is a country's borders. To keep terrorists from harming us, we screen visitors carefully, are properly suspicious of groups that want to destroy us, and guard our borders vigilantly. For our personal "homeland security" to work well, we have to be able to identify the enemy and take appropriate action.

Depending on our relationship to evil, we could shift from one image to another. We might keep malice locked up in a dank prison, paint our impulse toward mean-spiritedness into a corner or guard our borders against the intrusions of sexual terrorism. As you examine the walls around your moral house, you might ask yourself if you have constructed a good line of defense or one that is too easily breached.

Innocence and experience. The virtue of innocence affirms that we should know something about evil, but by analyzing it and choosing against it, not by experiencing it. When I ask my students if they think experience is the best teacher, they usually say yes. But what they mean is that after they have learned something in theory, the idea truly comes home in on-the-field application.

Of course, experiential learning without theory can be deadly. As Dominic LaRusso says, "Experience . . . is the worst teacher since it gives the test first and the lesson later. Learn by experience, for example, that iodine is poisonous to humans. . . . Worst yet, experience is a poor teacher since it offers no controls to guarantee the learning of good habits instead of bad."

As much as anything, this recognition of the role of experience is what distinguishes childhood innocence from adult innocence. Childhood innocence requires ignorance of evil. Once a child has a certain experience, part of innocence is lost, whether the choice was intentional or not. On her first day of kindergarten, my daughter Emily was chased by a boy who shouted at her, "I want to bite your butt!" In this moment, a line of language-innocence was crossed—and Emily could not "go back."

Adult innocence is not the same as ignorance. Like competent competitors, innocent adults know their opponent; they understand the shape and appeal of evil. They may even study evil, but they attempt to learn by observation, not by participation. Obviously, I don't have to lie to my colleagues to know that deceit is wrong, nor do I need to waste a year on the couch eating snacks to discover the problems with sloth. Our hope is to imitate Jesus, who, as Hebrews 4:15 says, was "tempted in every way, just as we are—yet he did not sin."

As we have seen, innocence is intimately connected with the good; it aims to set it free. At the same time, innocence has much to do with evil; it aims to restrict it. As it seeks to achieve these goals, innocence does its best to learn about evil by observation and analysis, not by experience.

WHAT INNOCENCE IS NOT

Three inadequate views of innocence tend to keep the virtue from being taken seriously by adults. At first glance, innocence sounds like perfection, like utterly undefiled wholesomeness. But *innocence is not the same as total purity*. We think this way when we are stuck in a childhood version of it. The virtue of innocence doesn't require perfection any more than any other virtue. A commitment to patience doesn't require perfect patience. When I am running late and I jam my finger in a door and can't find my car keys and spill chocolate on my pants, I usually get angry. Do I say, "Well, I've lost patience for good now"? No, I repent and give it another try. This is the same pattern we take toward innocence. Though we may "lose" it temporarily, it is not lost forever.

Most of us can remember a classmate in junior high who drove us crazy with niceness, who said of the resident thug (the one who slammed our locker shut every day and insisted we give him money), "Oh, he's just misunderstood." Though our smarmy class-mate probably received praise from teachers and parents, this kid is not the best model for innocence because *innocence is not a denial of pain and tragedy*. It is not a Precious Moments sentimentality. Though "childlikeness" is a quality often associated with innocence (as in Jesus' remarks in Mark 10:14-15 that the kingdom of God belongs to the little children), the praiseworthy quality of the child is not being sugar and spice and everything nice.

In fact, children are often upset when the villain doesn't get severely punished. Children "love justice," as Chesterton says.

Also, *innocence is not the same as gullibility*, a state of mind ripe for manipulation. As Kathleen Norris puts it, this is a false innocence, "the ignorance of those who should know better." Instead, virtuous innocence is a paradox of informed ignorance. A qualified knowledge of evil makes us better able to resist the seductions around us.

Parents reveal this perspective when they tell their children, "Don't get into a car with a stranger." In other words, "Don't be gullible. We want you to be innocent of the *experience* of being kidnapped but not of the *threat*." Because con artists (and some sarcastic jokesters) depend on the gullibility of those they dupe, we need to be more aware of the tricks of deceivers, not less aware. If Jesus admired air-headed naiveté, he would not have also told us to be "as shrewd as snakes."

In light of this understanding of what innocence is (our sense of justice that sets the good free and binds evil) and what it is not (total purity, sentimentality or gullibility), we can return to the problems innocence faces, including the ways evil is made to look attractive. In Psalm 73, Asaph envies the rich, who seem to prosper despite their arrogant wickedness. He states, "Surely in vain I have kept my heart pure and washed my hands in innocence" (v. 13). Asaph find himself "troubled . . . deeply" (v. 16)—and we may end up in the same place for a while, especially as we take in our culture's favorite storylines.

INNOCENCE SLAUGHTERED AND PACKAGED

Although Asaph's questions about innocence show how certain tensions are timeless, each era's dominant storytellers create their own versions of the attractions of losing innocence. Hollywood is not in a conspiracy to advance a wicked agenda, but certain themes in stories tend to get repeated in appealing ways.

Stories that show innocence as dull and inexperienced. From Clark Gable to the latest incarnation of James Bond, the suave and street-wise man—and, more recently, the aggressively romantic woman—typically outshines characters portrayed as the shy, unadventurous innocent. Those who are not boldly seductive or wildly dangerous, or not violating the boundaries of others, are often played as boring and unsophisticated—in a word, losers. Some TV shows regularly ridicule a character for his or her naiveté, portrayed as simple-headed dopiness or outright stupidity. It's the classic "straw man" argument: set up a lightweight version of the innocent behavior you oppose, then knock it over.

Behind the swagger is the assumption that "worldly" experience is what matters and, our culture tells us, "You can't criticize something you haven't experienced." This leaves the uninitiated without a shred of credibility to stand on. Of course, the argument is true in some circumstances. We shouldn't draw conclusions about a person from hearsay or complain about the taste of something we haven't tasted. I told my parents for years that I hated sour cream. Then one day I tried it.

But sour cream seems a long way from not being allowed to evaluate having a one-night stand because I haven't had one or to express outrage over a drunk-driving manslaughter because I haven't killed anyone.

Stories that show how innocence doesn't face "real life." Hollywood tells us that innocence is fine for children (ironically, they are often the rescuers in movies), but the rest of us get the message that we need to suck it up and see life as it is. Life is dark and gritty, full of deceit and insincerity and greed. That's why we begin with G-rated films and "progress" through PG, PG-13, on our way to R, because the more mature we are, the tougher the reality we can handle. Again, part of this perspective is true enough—and we need to tell the truth about oppression, decadence and brutality. At the same time, toddlers should not see gruesome murder mysteries any more than adults should be restricted to *Bippy the Bunny and the Agape Kids.*

Yet the "real life" presented on the screen is usually far from real. For the most part, real life is rather ordinary. My life isn't dreary—but it will not be coming soon to a theater near you. Stories on the screen are interesting to us precisely because they are *un*realistic: tragedy dripping with gory special effects or romance that is grossly overstated. I enjoy golden-glowing perfection as much as the next person, but my life is rarely accompanied by flattering lighting and a sexy soundtrack.

By the "leave innocence behind" logic, nothing that has occurred in human history should ever be hidden from us. But how does exposure to every terrible act profit us? Should everything that exists be seen or heard? Toilet duties are "real life." Hacking off an arm with a machete is "real life." So what? If some information is helpful, thrilling or moral, mustn't some information be harmful, dull or immoral?

Stories that show how losing innocence is required for Great Fun. Hollywood repeatedly celebrates one particular version of lost innocence, the classic "coming of age" story. Typically, Boy (not Girl) is unhappy and frustrated. Boy's lack of sexual experience makes him look like a failure—and the longer he's inexperienced, the more of a social misfit he becomes. Boy meets potential bedmate. Boy makes several mistakes but finally becomes a sexual "success." Boy is happy and no longer frustrated.

The argument in these films, such as it is, presents to the audience a singular path to adulthood: the loss of sexual innocence. But note the reasoning. Why is it that losing one's virginity is the most important part of "growing up"? What about becoming less narcissistic or more motivated to reduce social injustices?

Just as Herod's slaughtering of the innocents was a tragedy, so Hollywood's stories that slaughter innocence are tragic. The good news is that Herod was not entirely successful—and neither is

Hollywood. The Messiah survived then and he is with us today, helping us resist breaking the boundaries that protect innocence.

IF WE CAN LOSE OUR INNOCENCE, CAN WE ALSO FIND IT?

I have a confession to make. When my sister was about six years old, my brother and I took her around to the side of the house and told her there was no Santa Claus. I know, we were cruel and unfeeling. And mean. We tarnished my sister's childhood innocence just to feel powerful. She could never go back to that unspoiled state.

We hear a lot about lost innocence, but what is lost when we lose it? Some would say we lose the inhibitions that keep us from having fun. This familiar prejudice argues that heaven is dull and heaven's children are duller, sitting around playing harps all day. Why harps? Are there no guitars in heaven?

The more important issue here has to do with the long-term, good effects of innocence. Typically, we think in terms of *losing* innocence—and how we are permanently tarnished in the loss— but it might be more helpful to think of what is *gained* when innocence is *found*. In fact, what we lose when innocence is lost is actually a kind of reverse way of talking about what we find when innocence is found. So, I will phrase each "gain" positively.

Gaining the ability to experience pleasures wholeheartedly. Consider the possibilities around a dinner table. Bob has been overeating much of his life. He looks enviously at Too-Thin Tina, a recovering anorexic. Sam, of average weight, taps his fingers as he remembers what his physician said about food choices and his high cholesterol. Lisa smiles, gathers in every aroma, then holds out her hands to offer table grace: "Thank you, God, for all these terrific things, for sweet fruit and the greenness of peas. Thank you for all the variety we enjoy." Lisa says, "Amen," not realizing that she is the only one at the table who will truly take pleasure in the meal.

When the virtue of innocence is weak, appreciations for good things are reserved or contaminated. When innocence is strong, enjoyment can be thoroughly embraced. To understand this principle, we need to remember that all transgressions of the *virtue* of innocence involve immoral acts. (Having sex for the first time on one's wedding night is not a loss of the virtue of innocence. It is a loss of a childhood state of ignorance.) All losses of moral innocence diminish the fullness of joy in which a pleasure was meant to be experienced.

An innocent pleasurable experience has no tainted memory associated with it; it has no lingering recollection of twisting a good act into self-indulgence or vindictiveness. One friend, repeatedly exposed to pornography at an early age, struggles now, in his middle years, to see sex as tender communion with his wife. For him, sexual pleasure "needs to be" associated with something illicit. Guilt follows.

Spoiled innocence, when it takes over a life, leads to a thoroughgoing cynicism. We've seen it all and we aren't impressed. "Oh, you care about politics? Good for you." "Isabel just received a promotion? Who cares?" A disdain of all things innocent is a way of saying that nothing is worthy of our commitment. Wholesale cynicism moves us toward a kind of nothingness, a diminishing of self and a sense that others should vanish as well.

When spoiled innocence reaches a critical mass—or when we believe culture is unredeemable—we live in communal cynicism. Years ago, my working environment was marked by suspicion and anger. When I spoke up in a meeting, I felt as if a huge spotlight shone on me, exposing every flaw. Then a new supervisor came. I never imagined one person could so quickly change the whole tenor of a community. He maintained a kind of innocence about our mission and encouraged us in our daily tasks. As he did, trust and joy grew.

Gaining the reassuring security of unbreached borders. In the late eighth century, European emperor Charlemagne asked a councilor, Alcuin, to tutor his son, Pepin. To accomplish this task, Alcuin created a series of questions and answers for Pepin to memorize. The catechism included the following exchange:

Pepin: What is the liberty of man?
Alcuin: Innocence.

Alcuin recognized the relationship between secure moral thresholds and freedom. The self-indulgent try to convince us otherwise, but there's plenty of evidence to support Alcuin. Although it may appear to restrict freedom, innocence in fact creates a stability that leads to greater freedom.

Perhaps the most obvious example is the keeping of covenants. If a wife is secure in the innocence of her husband's faithfulness, she trusts him with greater freedom as he interacts with other women. If a student maintains the classroom covenant of not cheating, her professors are much more likely to trust her during an exam.

We can also see the importance of secure boundaries in neighborhoods, cities and nations. The greater the communal innocence, the greater the freedom. In a safe neighborhood, we might not even lock our houses. But if a sexual predator moves in next door, we snap the deadbolts shut. A culture that, on the whole, values healthy norms will find it easier to remain innocent regarding the violation of those norms. When I was young, my first exposure to a photograph of a naked woman was in an eighth-grade biology textbook—and I was not raised in the church. I suspect that today, few eighth-grade boys, in or out of the church, have not been exposed to hard-core pornography on the Internet. But not all social norms are "going downhill." In the 1960s, racist remarks were permitted, even encouraged. Today, our communal innocence won't tolerate this kind of discrimination, so it is easier for all of us to avoid vicious words, to not even think them.

Once borders are breached, forgiveness and recovery are possible, but they may prove difficult. Rebuilding a secure wall takes time. Since innocence is a choice, we are all day long deciding if we will keep our borders in good repair, if we will learn of evil without experiencing it. We need to remember that every hour we make these choices is a good hour. The voice of the Liar tells us that these choices don't really matter, that once the border has been transgressed, we are now "damaged goods."

But this is a lie, because innocence is a virtue, not a "once and done" phenomenon. Too many of us feel that once we have become drunk or stolen merchandise or cheated, we might as well continue to give in. We act as if being disciplined no longer matters. But it does! If we were in a military battle, would we throw open the doors of the fortress because part of a wall came down? No, we would repair the wall and say, "Never surrender!" The prophet Micah might have us add, "Do not gloat over me, my enemy! Though I have fallen, I will rise. Though I sit in darkness, the LORD will be my light" (7:8).

And make no mistake: though a border gets repaired, the broken wall is part of our history—and that's okay. One woman told me the story of how she suffered sexual abuse when she was young. All her life she had been attempting to "re-experience" her lost childhood, to go back and find the feeling of innocence before it got crushed. But our hope is not in retracing our steps to find what was lost, because it won't change anything to pretend we are back in kindergarten or at summer camp or in a family of gentle, loving souls. Our innocence is not hidden somewhere, waiting to be found. It is in us, by God's grace, waiting to be transformed.

Gaining a heightened sense of justice. Because innocence is a child of justice, a strengthened virtue of innocence produces a more mature ability to separate the just from the blameworthy. We also become more willing to speak out against injustice. When Jesus says, "Blessed are the pure in heart, for they will see God"

(Matthew 5:8), I think he means it proportionally: the purer we are, the more we will *see* God, that is, see him at work in circumstances around us, see life as he sees it, recognize what God calls just or unjust.

During World War II, the village of Le Chambon near Vichy, France, became known as the safest place on the continent for Jewish refugees. The leader of the town, Pastor André Trocmé, influenced others with a sense of justice borne of his passion to protect the innocent. He fed them, often going hungry himself. Though Nazis constantly pressured him to obey orders to name and locate Jews in the area, Trocmé refused, and led thousands of Jews to Switzerland. Biographer Peter Hallie says, "He believed that 'decent' people who stay inactive out of cowardice or indifference when around them human beings are being humiliated and destroyed are the most dangerous people in the world. His nonviolence was not passive or saccharine, but an almost brutal force for awakening human beings." Trocmé expected a dedicated innocence to result in a zeal for justice.

Likewise, the loss of innocence may reduce the "gumption" that justice requires. We tend to downplay the immorality of what we do not resist. If we have transgressed boundaries concerning revenge, we may struggle to forgive others. If we have habitually lied, we probably won't defend the importance of the truth. If we have lost innocence through gossip, we find it difficult to practice the justice of protecting another's reputation. If we have lost innocence through promiscuity, we may find it difficult to pursue sexual justice. Our sense of justice matters, and innocence is tightly wrapped up in it.

❧ THE DISCIPLINE OF ADVOCACY

As I mentioned when I defined innocence, we don't have to stretch our imagination much to see life in the terms of a court-room. The phrase "life is a trial" comes to our lips or ears with regularity. Extending the metaphor, don't we feel we are "in the dock" at times, as if under attack by a team of prosecuting attorneys?

"Do you swear to tell the truth, the whole truth, and every itsy-weensy bit of truth?"

"Sure."

"Have you ever considered lying about your employer?"

"Who hasn't?"

"Given her recent rudeness, don't you think that now would be a good time to make up a juicy one?"

"Well, um, I guess so—"

Sometimes in the trial of life, we are innocent, but we hear voices and arguments pushing us to be unfaithful. How should we respond? Thankfully, Jesus showed the way. In the wilderness, the accuser challenged him to abuse his power, deny his spiritual loyalties and reduce God to a carnival trick. When asked in these ways to transgress his innocence, Jesus defended his commitments. He knew what he believed and could cite scriptural support.

When a temptation to break our innocence comes, we can pray, and we can also exercise our reason. This kind of advocacy can be seen as a spiritual discipline. In the context of justice, and our legal system, who protects innocence? An advocate. Who exposes the guilty? Though lawyers have a soiled reputation these days, the falsely accused surely want the best defense. And remember, one name for the Holy Spirit is "the Advocate," because he testifies for Jesus and intercedes on our behalf (John 14:26; 15:26).

As a spiritual discipline, advocacy is a reasoned defense of innocence; it is the practice of making a case against false accusers. Though we usually think of an advocate as someone who speaks on behalf of someone else, I am thinking of the ways we can be an advocate for our own spiritual vitality. When our innocence is at risk, we can plead our case with good arguments and solid evidence. We can learn to be bold enough to say to our accusers what Job said of his: "Your maxims are proverbs of ashes; your defenses are defenses of clay" (13:12).

What are the qualities of a good advocate? If we were actually in court, we would want an attorney who is knowledgeable, a tireless researcher, a superb arguer, an insightful thinker and a compassionate lover of justice. We would want a clear-minded strategist who presents ideas eloquently, and someone not afraid to ask hard questions.

Let's suppose your roommate won't do the dishes or pick up wet towels or put away old mail. You've asked Evan to do these things. Nicely. Several times. You leave smiley-faced notes on the mirror to no avail. As your anger percolates, certain rationalizations toward evil resound in your head: *I have every right to be angry. The next time Evan comes home, I ought to blow my top! Don't back down!*

When voices like these plead with us to lose our temper, we should defend our innocence. We could say, *I may be within my rights to rage at Evan, but anger will probably just draw out more anger. I need to remember Ephesians 4:31: "Get rid of all bitterness, rage and anger, brawling and slander, along with every form of malice."* Making a defense isn't foolproof, but it is a good strategy.

Many biblical sources affirm the importance of advocacy. In addition to Jesus' brilliance in the desert during his temptation, Paul skillfully makes his case for the gospel in Romans. Another resource can be found in Proverbs 7. In this chapter, a father teaches his son about the dangers of sexual seduction. As you read the following excerpts, imagine the father showing the red-light district to his son:

> My son, . . . store up my commands within you. . . . At the window of my house . . . I noticed . . . a youth who had no sense. He was going down the street near her corner, walking along in the direction of her house. . . . Then out came a woman to meet him, dressed like a prostitute and with crafty intent. . . . She took hold of him and kissed him and . . . said . . . "Come, . . . let's enjoy ourselves with love! My husband is not at home. . . ." With persuasive words she led him astray. (vv. 1, 6-8, 10, 13, 18-19, 21)

Above all, notice how the father wants his son to move from childhood ignorance to adult innocence. He wants his son to know what evil is like and how it attempts to convince. The son should know about prostitution—but not by experience.

And what does the father offer as resources for his son? How is the son to fend off the seduction? First, he tells his son to have clear goals, to remember his words and commands. Don't be ignorant: know what it is you are trying to retain and to protect. Next, he says, in essence, "Be wise. Know the innocence-breaker's nonverbal and verbal schemes. Be prepared to reject weak arguments." In the terms I have set out, the father wants his son to learn to be a good advocate for his own innocence, to know the opposing side and how to marshal a case against it. That's what Jesus did in the wilderness. He was a skillful advocate against his accuser. And he prayed.

The virtue of innocence is protected, in part, by a discipline of advocacy that is willing to challenge what attacks it. And maintaining our innocence has more benefits than we might imagine. We can experience pleasures more wholeheartedly, live freely within more secure borders and manifest a stronger sense of justice. Perhaps it is time to attend to innocence. As in Herod's era, perhaps it is time for a little weeping and wailing.

FOR DISCUSSION OR REFLECTION

1. G. K. Chesterton says, "Children are innocent and love justice while most of us are wicked and naturally prefer mercy." Connect this idea to your own experience.

2. If innocence is "our sense of justice that sets good things free and binds up evil," what good things do you habitually set free? How have you bound up evil without being bound by it?

3. Can you think of a time when your innocence was "slaughtered" by Hollywood?

4. What stories do you know that show innocence as dull and backward, show how innocence can't face "real life" or show how losing innocence is great fun?

5. How does the idea that innocence is a virtue relate to your self-talk when you think of yourself as "damaged goods"?

6. "What is lost when innocence is lost" was rephrased as "what is gained when innocence is practiced." Discuss examples in each area: gaining the ability to experience pleasure wholeheartedly; gaining the reassuring security of unbreached borders; and gaining a heightened sense of justice.

EXERCISE

With a small group or a friend you can trust, discuss areas in which you struggle to maintain your innocence. Share with each other the choices you tend to make when your innocence is threatened. Invite your friend to evaluate your choices. Thinking of yourselves as members of a law firm hired to defend this innocence, practice advocacy: help each other to "mount a defense."

1. What Scriptures are important in the defense?

2. What are the best arguments against your accusers (and seducers), and the best arguments in favor of the innocent choices you want to maintain?

Pledge to check back in a week or so to discuss the ways you acted as an advocate for your innocence.

4 ❧ AUTHENTICITY

our genuine longing

A thinking man should always attack the strongest thing in his own time. For the strongest thing of the time is always too strong.

G. K. CHESTERTON

For about fifteen years, my parents were alcoholics, drinking to drunkenness every night. I detested their glazed eyes and slurred speech, but I think my worst memories relate to smell: the sluggish sweetness of bourbon, the stale stench of my mom's unwashed nylons, the sudden bolt of mold when I lifted the lid from a pot left on the stove.

One afternoon I received a call that my mom was in the hospital, jaundiced from her pickled liver. Though I didn't want to go see her, I played the dutiful son. At her bedside I thought she looked so ghostly she might die right in front of me.

But she didn't. Day by day, she recovered and stopped drinking. On one level, it didn't matter. Physically the alcohol had done its damage. She deteriorated for eight years, finally succumbing to cirrhosis.

During this period of my life and to the present—though my

dad became sober—I have had to contend with many consequences of my parents' choices. One pattern in particular went
unnoticed for a long time. Throughout my adolescence and early
marriage, I did what many do in an alcoholic family: I smiled.

It's not that I was always happy or that I was just trying to put
the best face on things. Instead, my smiling was how I learned to
cope with the outside world through deception, maintaining a fa-
çade that everything was "just fine." As much as anything in my
life, this experience moved me to care about authenticity. Why?
Because I had lived a lie—and I hated it.

OUR LONGING FOR SINCERITY

I wonder, are current conditions in American culture prompting
us to smile to our detriment? More than ever, we seem to have
given ourselves over to the superficial values of face-tightening
makeovers and the garish illusions of Las Vegas. Despite these
seductions—or because of them—we end up longing for the real,
even though we are not sure what "being real" means.

Weary of phoniness. Everywhere we turn, the counterfeit con-
fronts us. We see imitation boulders on the boardwalk. A National
Geographic DVD ad says, "Come face to face with rock antelope.
. . . Wander through . . . yellow columbine." In my living room?
Who are they kidding? In the chapter on discernment, I discussed
how the Velveteen Rabbit Factor, our inability to determine what
is real, leads us to abdicate our responsibility toward discernment.
Here I want to draw attention to how the phoniness in our world
feeds us empty calories—and leads us to desire something more
nutritious, more authentic.

Sometimes we feel betrayed. At first, we believe that a story, a
building or a person is "real," then we suffer disappointment when
we discover how much is contrived. Automated voices tell us they
value our business or that our "call is important. Please stay on
the line." But if I'm so valuable, why am I on hold for twenty min-

utes, listening to a repetitive loop of banality? All of this fakery accumulates like barnacles on the hull of our soul.

And we are tired of being served the cheese sandwich of niceness. It's not that we want incivility or boorishness. It's just that, after a while, we're not sure we can trust all the pleasantries. At church everyone smiles so sweet and nice but, when we stop to think about it, we haven't had a conversation of substance for months. We have dozens (hundreds!) of "friends" on Facebook but no one to ask to coffee when we need to talk. Occasionally, a genuine human encounter takes place, and we are taken aback by the solid feel of the moment and by the contrast with our more typical clichés. We search for the real, the really real, anything that will make us think meaningfully or act creatively or feel known.

So we watch reality TV, that paradoxical world of scripted unscriptedness in which "real" contestants *perform* for the camera. We yearn for reality, even fake reality. Yet our channel surfing shows how bored we are. We want to be startled with something that moves us, something that pushes into our lives in a consequential way. Perhaps this is one reason we are so attracted to sex and violence in the media. We want an experience that reminds us we are alive. We are desperate to feel fully real, fully authentic.

Struggling with duplicity. Though weary of phoniness, we are also lured in by the attractions of living multiple, contradictory lives. We are pious with our Jesus friends but loose and crude with our party friends. As creatures in a consumer culture, we just do what others do, because being accepted and admired seems far more important than being authentic. In a print ad for jewelry, a topless woman crosses her arms over her substantial breasts, highlighting the giant stones in her rings and necklace. The print reads, "Who cares if they aren't real?" Often we don't.

Duplicity is hard to avoid. In my role as professor, I write many letters of recommendation. With a few students, I wonder, How can I be genuine when these letters are so typically inflated? Should I write with the standard hyperbole of our times? Then there is the deceit we observe or suspect in others. Don't we all have friends that on some level we aren't sure we can trust? Their compliments feel insincere, forced, patronizing. They entrust us with their scathing remarks about others, so much so that we can't help but think we are the butt of their gossip when they are with others. And when we share genuine sorrows, they nod in sympathy. Then their cell phone rings, and they excuse themselves.

Sometimes we recognize our own embellishment of the truth, the way we falsify details so our neighbors will think better of us. Maybe the most common lie on a college campus is, "Oh yes, I know what you're talking about." We'd rather lie than risk damage to our reputation. Insecurity hounds us, so we throw something— anything—out there to keep it at bay. We're just spinning things positively, right? We all need to sell ourselves, right? In a world that blesses exaggeration, we do what it takes to compete, to keep up with everybody else's exaggerations.

We're torn. We see and object to phoniness. We see and fall into degrees of duplicity. Yet in the midst of this cultural noise, if we listen well, we can hear a still small voice reminding us of who we really are and how we are coming across to others. We sigh and lean toward this voice because, despite our insecurities, we want to be accepted and loved as we are.

A BIBLICAL PRIMER ON AUTHENTICITY

The Bible has been called the most honest, most earthy of holy books. Noah gets drunk. David commits adultery and covers it up with murder. One of Jesus' hand-picked disciples rats him out while the others fight over who gets to be first in line at heaven's party. Whatever criticism the Scriptures might deserve, "sanitizing the saints" is not one of them.

In fact, part of what makes Jesus compelling is his straightforwardness. He means what he says and says what needs to be heard. When he is twelve and his parents can't find him, they search till they catch up to him at a synagogue. Mary and Joseph wag their fingers and tell Jesus never to leave their sight again. Jesus bursts into tears, grabs his mother's hand and dutifully honors his parents all the way home.

Of course, Jesus does no such thing. He says, "Why were you searching for me? Didn't you know I had to be in my Father's house?" (Luke 2:49). Based on my experience as a dad, I'm guessing Mary and Joseph weren't entirely pleased by Jesus' bluntness. They might have been thinking, *Couldn't you at least have told us where you were going?*

But our Lord spoke the truth genuinely. When Peter gives him unsolicited, non-faith-based advice, Jesus says, "Get behind me, Satan!" (Matthew 16:23). When his anguish on Gethsemane weighs on him, he cries out, "My Father, if it is possible, may this cup be taken from me" (26:39). What words could be more authentic? Here is the Son of God speaking out of his convictions and his emotional state. Unlike many churchgoers, Jesus the Messiah does not feel the burden to appear invincible.

Not only does Jesus model sincerity, he reserves his harshest criticism for the insincerity of religious leaders: "Woe to you, teachers of the law and Pharisees, you hypocrites! You clean the outside of the cup and dish, but inside they are full of greed and self-indulgence" (Matthew 23:25). In Jesus' vision of the faithful life, the inside and the outside both matter. As disciples, we are called to be consistent, to have our "outside" good actions come from corresponding "inside" motivations. Refraining from murdering is not enough for holiness; our anger matters. Not committing adultery is insufficient; the lust in our minds matters.

Just when we think we are nice people, good people, Jesus takes discipleship to the level of inner life. Frankly, I find this unnerving. Jesus' criticism names me because my actual faith is so much less impressive than my public presentation. Whatever the virtue of authenticity means, it must include a willingness to be straightforward and a sensitivity to our own intentions.

AUTHENTICITY AT A GLANCE

So, what is authenticity? Should I stare deeply into a mirror until I find my true self? Philosopher Charles Taylor, while defending a version of "being true to ourselves," says that one problem with our culture is that it wants to use the self as the only guide to fulfilling the self. Instead, he says, "I can define my identity only against the background of things that matter."

At the same time, "finding our true self" *is* relevant because some of us, maybe all of us, would be better off if we more thoroughly knew our strengths and understood our weaknesses. But we need to be careful. We would be using the wrong map if we only took that road to authenticity. Our "authentic destination" is not a perfectly centered self. We are better off using synonyms such as *sincerity* or *genuineness*.

Another reason to resist a self-searching view of authenticity is our culture's overstated platitude "Just follow your heart." This advice seems especially pertinent to outnumbered soldiers, lovelorn geeks and all underdogs involved in any sort of athletic competition. That's fine. But what if our heart tells us to have an affair, sink our retirement funds into the lottery or betray a friend? I admit, sometimes we need more passion for pursuing good things or enough moxie to get out of a deadening routine. But "following your heart" is not a magic ax that will cut a clear path through the wilderness of our decisions. Whatever happened to "follow wisdom" or "follow Jesus"?

Given these considerations, I define authenticity as *a rigorous inside-out consistency that courageously cares for others*. Let's take a look at each phrase in this definition.

An inside-out consistency. On one hand, the most common-

place interpretation is, "Have integrity. Be who you say you are."
True enough. We should not be hypocrites. We should not say
we are "humbled by your praise" and then puff ourselves up like
a mating prairie chicken. We should not say, "I'll pray for you,"
and then not pray.

On the other hand, we could turn some of this inside-out thinking upside-down by saying, "There are no hypocrites; we all live
according to our beliefs." If you want to characterize my worldview, my theology, my philosophy of life, simply observe my life. I
will in my (speech and other) choices show you what I believe. If
I talk as if only the natural world exists, am I revealing that I don't
strongly believe in the supernatural?

Another aspect of the "inside-outness" of authenticity is that
not only should we "*be* what we *say*" but we should "*say* what we
do." When called upon, we should use words that are consistent
with our other actions. Though the phrase "actions speak louder
than words" is often true, it misses the point that, at times, the
thing most necessary is the "action" of speech. If in my heart I love
you, does it really matter that I say it aloud? My wife tells me yes!
If the thing most helpful is encouragement or admonishment or
brainstorming, I should speak, and not merely let my silent actions do the talking.

A rigorous commitment. The word *rigorous* adds heft because,
without it, a response might be, "How obvious! Who doesn't know
that we shouldn't be hypocrites?" And, clearly, there *is* some dull
straightforwardness in every definition of virtue, because the difficulty is much more in the living than in the knowing. In our attempts to live authentically, the word *rigorous* heightens the sense
of scrutiny; it reminds us that authenticity is hard work. Perhaps
I am only playing the martyr when I make a "sincere" offer of help:
"Of course I'll vacuum this month." Sigh. Or perhaps my "genuine" admission of weakness is actually a plot to elicit praise: "I
must be the worst employee ever. What do you think?" True au-

thenticity requires tough-minded analysis.

Plato put it this way: "Grant that all external possessions be in harmony with my inner man." Many have summarized this as, "Let the inner and the outer person meet." I love this idea, this challenge. When someone listens to us or sees our outward actions, they should know that—except for playful teasing—our choices truly represent who we are, that our assertions testify accurately to inner conclusions. In George MacDonald's delightful story *The Princess and Curdie*, the main character, Curdie, is given a special talent such that when he feels the hand of someone, he can tell if the person is becoming more angelic or more beastly. He might hold the hand of an outwardly beautiful person only to feel a gnarled claw. Once, when Curdie touched the paw of a hideous creature, a patchwork of vulture, elephant and tiger, he felt the hand of a child. Curdie wondered if he could "pull the child out of the beast!" Later, when the wise princess of the story rested her hand in Curdie's, he recognized that her outer flesh-glove was the same as the inner real hand. Her authenticity was absolute. She lived so genuinely and purely that her inner and outer person met.

Part of the rigor of authenticity can be seen in Jesus' variation on Plato's inner/outer theme. When discussing insincere oath making, Jesus says, "Simply let your 'Yes' be 'Yes,' and your 'No,' 'No'" (Matthew 5:37 NIV). We don't need to add flashy assurances to our statements if we truly mean what we say. Part of being authentic is being dependable, morally predictable. Ironically, we tend to be conformist in practice (all wearing jeans) while being nonconformist in principles (holding to widely divergent ideas about honesty). On the contrary, we should be personally flexible but morally predictable. We should hold to similar important values and then apply them in wide-ranging, freedom-inspired ways. To get to this place, we will need to be much more aware of our commitments, more willing to talk about the choices that reflect our beliefs.

We might begin by being more rigorously authentic in our daily communication. In a culture enamored with clichéd overstatements, this is tough. Of course, words can be interpreted in endless ways and are understood in context. But wouldn't it be refreshing to hear "partially" when things aren't really "totally," or "pleasant" when things aren't truly "awesome"? When we describe dessert as "wicked" or "sinfully decadent," don't those terms lose some of their biblical power? True authenticity should lead us to more meaningful speech.

Courageous concern. Courage is the parent virtue of authenticity. It takes courage to tell the truth, to be genuine, to resist the falsifications that our peer groups endorse. To be sincere when others are being ruthlessly sarcastic isn't easy. And "care for others" must inform our actions. Authenticity can be misunderstood, misapplied or used to justify all manner of interpersonal violence. Like all virtue, authenticity can but should not be made a god unto itself. We should not use our commitment to sincerity as an excuse for blasting everyone who gets in our way, like those pedestrians who take their sweet time in a crosswalk when we are in a hurry. Know what I mean?

Authenticity is not "cruel honesty," as if we are justified saying whatever is on our minds. Being genuine does not mean that we spew up every observation we make. Sometimes, claims to authenticity are no more than excuses for being vindictive. "I'm only saying this to be helpful. You are really fat." True authenticity practices a gracious honesty—and it takes wisdom to know when is the best time to say the fullness of what we think and feel. This view keeps us from making the mistake that because we *feel* genuine, we must be practicing the virtue of authenticity. What really matters is how we live out authentic actions in the presence of others.

Authenticity is also not indulgent transparency, as if we are always noble for divulging our darkest secrets. A young woman came into my office years ago and told me her story of sexual abuse and suicidal depression. I felt honored that she trusted me—until I learned that she had been revealing every pity-inspiring detail to everyone in the building, one person after another. She was compulsively transparent. And while transparency may sometimes be called for, especially in intimate relationships and during confession, it is not a justification for undisciplined speech.

Curiously, authenticity doesn't mean we ought never act insincerely. "Pretending" is, at times, essential, inevitable and ethical. In *Faking It*, William Ian Miller acknowledges that although insincerity conjures up many negative connotations, "I am not a hypocrite . . . for pretending to find interesting what is dull, . . . [n]or am I a hypocrite for putting on a somber face at the news of the untimely death of a person I didn't especially care for." Should we "authentically" act out our resentment for our coworker, our jealousy for our friend's success or our desires to break a confidence? Miller's term "faking it" might feel repugnant to us, but we regularly practice it more than we might like to admit. Don't parents often force their children to say "I'm sorry"? Then they add, "Now say it again, this time like you mean it." When you find yourself mainly noticing certain body parts of someone on the beach, do you "fake" like you are observing their anatomy differently? Probably, like me, you do.

Rather than characterizing these choices as "faking it," I prefer C. S. Lewis's idea: "Let us pretend in order to make the pretense into a reality." One age-old question is, which comes first, the attitude or the behavior? Researchers have discovered that when we make an angry facial expression, we actually start to feel angry, which suggests that action might change attitude more than we realize. And we all know that if we had to wait for an absolutely pure virtuous impulse in order to act, there would be little virtue indeed.

Suppose my neighbor Joan thinks she is the only one who should be permitted to park in front of her house—on the street, the *public* street. When she sees a visitor of mine parking there, Joan storms toward me and lets loose with expletive-laced threats. On one hand, I authentically want to smack her all the way back to her own yard. On the other hand, I authentically want to keep my anger from getting the best of me. My second impulse is just as sincere as the first, though in the moment I struggle to fulfill it. Lewis says I should act lovingly toward Joan. In doing so, not only will I be a better neighbor in the short run, I will, over time, actually grow into the love that I'm pretending to have. How else could I love my enemies? Practicing authenticity requires courage and love. In addition to difficult neighbors, many obstacles arise.

BEING REAL IS A REAL PROBLEM

When I was a boy, I spent many afternoons with my legs straddling a wide, white branch of a walnut tree. I fingered the dials and wheels of the plywood instrument panel I knew would one day take my brother and me to Mars. During dreamy summer days, when we weren't throwing rotten walnuts at each other, we might pose any number of profound questions, such as, "How long would it take to fry an ant with a magnifying glass?" But our favorite question was, "If you had to choose, would you rather go blind or deaf?" The answer could not have been more obvious to me then. I would rather go deaf, sight being too precious to lose. For the sighted, seeing is usually the most defining sense.

How much more true now. In an image-saturated culture, what could be more important than sight? Unfortunately, we have come to believe that seeing is the highest measure of all things. This is what I call the gospel of sight, that what the eye values is the most important truth, that the image—our image—is what matters most. Our language hints at this, with its common vision metaphors: "I *see* what you mean, and I'll *focus* on it, *view* it through a *lens*, with my mind's *eye*, to *frame* it."

Though I don't dislike the media (I love movies; I watch too

much TV), I take G. K. Chesterton's observation at the start of this
chapter to heart—that "the strongest thing of the time is always
too strong"—and I see "the strongest thing" as the way images
have influenced our thoughts and behavior. I began this chapter
with a reference to my parents' alcoholism. I hope you can't directly relate to that specific. On another level, perhaps we are all
addicts. We are drunk on images and their effects.

The gospel of sight and appearances. Most commercials say that
all that matters is being beautiful and young and thin and fit. And
ripped with tight abs. How can we be deeply authentic if we think
that how we look should be our top priority? Of course, caring about
our appearance is not unimportant or "beneath us." God made us to
notice beauty and appreciate style. We each have our own personal
way of being, our God-given idiosyncrasies, some of which have to
do with the way we present ourselves. Even so, our culture has
grossly overstated the role of the image. As elderly exercise guru
Jack LaLanne says, "I can't die. It would ruin my image."

We are outside-in focused, instead of inside-out. Parents have
said for years that it's what's on the inside that counts, but their
voices are drowned out by the thousands of voices we all hear
every day to the contrary. The gospel of sight says that everything
in our future rests on our attractiveness. In an ad for running
shoes, a woman admiring herself wants it both ways. The print
says, "She knows true beauty comes from the inside—but she
doesn't mind finding it in the mirror."

Inevitably, this outside-in orientation makes our sense of self
dependent on external forces. We need to be noticed, to be admired for our appearance. We conspire to get fed that attention,
though we know that flattery is thin soup indeed. Over a century
ago, Henry Ward Beecher got it right: "Clothes do not make the
man, but once he is made, they greatly improve his appearance."

We end up suffering from a perfectionism made worse by digi-
tal technology. Every commercial photograph of a face or body is

altered, enhanced, made visually stunning. Yet the more perfect the image, the greater the distance from our imperfect lives. This disparity discourages and corrupts us, especially women. It's hard enough to live up to a good friend's beauty; how does one compare to a digitalized "perfection" that even the supermodel doesn't possess? Some bury their guilt in starvation diets and persistent self-deprecation.

The gospel of sight and the preference for illusion. One Christmas, my wife and younger daughters and I visited my eldest daughter who, at that time, was living in St. Petersburg, Russia. After navigating through the rather grim city for eight days (including getting robbed on the Metro), I was delighted to spend the next five days in London before returning home to California. I said, "Ah, London is wonderful; it's like Disneyland." Ouch. Shouldn't I have said that Disneyland is like London? Somehow, the faux reality of Disneyland has burrowed into my head as the higher standard of excellence.

The gospel of sight's standard of illusion has a way of sneaking into everyday life. If the norms for the speed of romance are adopted from film, we will see our own efforts as plodding. When nature television becomes the norm for nature, real nature just doesn't measure up. It's not populated with enough "cute" or "fierce" beasts, nor do the wild things perform for us as they should. Perhaps our experience with illusions makes being authentic more difficult. We're uncomfortable in the wilderness of genuineness.

We often prefer illusion. Journalist Kiku Adatto says this orientation makes a curious kind of sense because "in a media-conscious environment, . . . authenticity means being the master of your own artificiality." We value being "authentically" in tune with certain fashionable pretenses, such as plastic surgery or bogus self-marketing. But why would a fake authenticity become more attractive? Charles Williams's cautionary thriller *Descent into Hell* provides some insight. He tells the story of middle-aged Lawrence Wentworth, who has a romantic crush on a much younger woman, Adela. In Williams's supernatural scheme, Wentworth's desire for Adela is so strong that, once Adela rejects him, he "creates" an illusion of Adela that caters to his every desire. One evening, during a torrential rain, the real Adela shows up at his door and asks to be let in. Wentworth looks at the phantom Adela in his room and then out at the real one, wet and cold, needing to be carried out of the rain. Williams says, "He recognized well enough that the real Adela might have given him considerable trouble to lift, but his whole damnation was that he would not choose the trouble to lift the real Adela."

I have been haunted by this line for years. What and who are the "real Adelas" in our lives that we refuse to carry? When do we dwell in our imagined ideal and ignore the plain truth in front of us—or inside us? To care for others with a rigorous inside-out consistency, we have to possess the courage to face, among other things, tragic realities. When friends of ours are in great pain, physical or otherwise, we often keep our distance because we feel awkward, because we don't know what to say. But in order to "lift" these real burdens, sometimes all we need to do, as some have said, is "show up." Being authentic includes being genuinely sad for others and carrying them as we are able.

At my college, I sometimes hear students say (after the revelation of an immoral event), "I can't believe that could happen at Westmont." I think, *Why? Do you not know that Westmont is inhabited by people?* Many of us prefer the illusion that followers of Jesus always lead outwardly better lives, that they always have superior marriages, more fulfilling jobs, less tragedy. We would be better off telling the truth about our humanity, even the terrible truths.

As we grow increasingly comfortable with the gospel of sight, we may find that we are more concerned with creating ourselves

than with knowing ourselves. If we alter our outer selves inces-
santly, we inevitably alter our inner selves, affirming a commercial version of the Good Life. With our souls in an illusory gated
community, safe from uncomfortable realities, we may feel the
need to separate ourselves from friends who tell us disagreeable
truths, especially truths about ourselves. And since we know how
far we are from the image we present, we know others are distant
also and so, ironically, we don't trust them.

Living in the age of the image is often thrilling and pleasing.
But when its qualities overwhelm instead of enrich—when the
gospel of sight reigns supreme—authenticity is threatened. The
loud and flashy world shouts down this quieter virtue. A sincere
effort will be required of us if we hope to be more genuine.

❧ THE DISCIPLINE OF REAL PRESENCE

More than once, you've probably had the aggravating experience of chatting away with a friend only to discover that she or he has not been listening to a thing you've said. The friend is "there" but "not there." We expect others to be present with us, and we know the difference this presence makes. As I see it, the idea of "real presence" provides good guidance for authenticity. In Roman Catholic tradition, it refers to the miraculous way Christ becomes manifest during the Eucharist. I want to adapt this idea so that we think of real presence as a way of being fully, sincerely in the moment, modeled after Jesus' way of being with his disciples.

Practicing real presence before God. I wonder how different my life would be if I acted as if I really believed God is with me at all times. Too often I catch myself doing or saying something that I would never do if a "real person" were in my presence. Although God is the Real Person who is there, my sense of his presence is not always enough to influence my behavior. This disturbs me, and I worry that these choices are the truest measure of my faith.

So I am encouraged when I read David's authenticity in the Psalms. He tells God just what is on his mind. He doesn't "pretty things up" with pious phrases and empty godtalk. In Psalm 42:3, he says, "My tears have been my food day and night, while people say to me all day long, 'Where is your God?'" Walter Wink characterizes this way of speaking: "Biblical prayer is impertinent, persistent, shameless, indecorous. It is more like haggling in an outdoor bazaar than the polite monologues of the churches." These perspectives embolden me to state genuinely to God my doubts and unchurch-like thoughts. He does not demand uninterrupted blissful worship. He knows better.

So let us practice authenticity in his real presence. We can cry out to God in all our agony—and we can use all the words we would use with a good friend. Our Good Friend can take it. He's heard it all before. One idea is to follow the structure of a psalm, filling in the categories with our own thoughts and feelings in the moment. Here are a few suggestions drawn out of David's Psalm 42:

- "These things I remember as I pour out my soul" (v. 4). We boldly state the issues, accusations or crises that we can't get out of our head.

- "Why, my soul, are you downcast?" (v. 5). We explore the nature of our discouragement.

- "I say to God my Rock, 'Why have you forgotten me?'" (v. 9). We are direct, wholly truthful as we talk with God, expressing the depths of our doubts.

- "Put your hope in God, for I will yet praise him, my Savior and my God" (v. 11). We conclude with authentic hope, reminding ourselves of what we would like to be and do.

Being authentic with God is essential. As we grow in transparency before the One who can see into our soul, we mature in other areas of genuineness.

Practicing real presence before the self. One would think that the person I would be least likely to fool with my own insincerities would be my very own self. When I look into the mirror and say that I should be a professional basketball star, I know I'm just dreaming. But not all our fantasies are so easily recognized.

The phrase "delusions of grandeur" exists because of our capacity for self-deception. Some of our delusions are harmless fantasies—as long as we don't obsess over them. Then again, some of our delusions are downright lies. We may have convinced ourselves we are the envy of all romantic lovers or that we are despicable little worms. To be authentic before the self, we probably need to check our self-perceptions with others' perceptions of us. After all, "the heart is deceitful above all things" (Jeremiah 17:9).

We can be remarkably unskilled in knowing ourselves. One of my friends moved to Park City, Utah, to become a snowboarding instructor, even though she had never snowboarded in her life. Students who barely pass my classes tell me they want to pursue doctoral work. Nonstop talkers say they are careful listeners. On the flip side, terrific writers say they can't put two sentences together, and sensitive souls call themselves callous. How can we become more aware and therefore more authentic?

Solitude encourages real presence with ourselves. Solitude is more than being silent; it means being alone in an intentional way, without music or television or conversation, without busyness of any kind. It means living in silence long enough to hear that part of ourselves that we work so hard to cover up. Blaise Pascal says that "the sole cause of man's unhappiness is that he does not know how to stay quietly in his own room." When we are truly alone, Pascal says, we discover our "wretchedness," and therefore our need for a Savior. Into our acknowledged darkness, Jesus comes robed in light.

In addition to solitude, because we are not especially skilled at seeing ourselves accurately, we could use an image-consciousness fairy. Just what you were expecting, right? Here's some background: In an all-college variety show years ago, the master of ceremonies made his grand entrance from the back of the audience, crooning like a second-rate lounge singer. He winked. He preened. He pointed at lovely ladies in that arrogant come-hither way. As he made his way to the stage, cheerleaders jumped for joy, and his full name lit up on the wall at the back of the stage.

From offstage came a voice, "Hey you!"

The emcee said, "What do you want?"

"I'm the image-consciousness fairy. My job is to cut through all the posturing and remind you that you are not the center of the universe."

"I'm not?"

"No. In fact, you are not even the center of this show. You are the emcee. You are supposed to draw attention to the other acts, not to yourself."

"Oh."

Though this scene was performed to get a laugh, I am convinced that we would all be more authentic if we each had an image-consciousness fairy in our lives. And we can have one, if we ask a friend to play this role for us. Do you know someone who will speak the truth about you to you? Are you willing to give another person the freedom to challenge and confront you? Proverbs 9:8 says, "Do not rebuke mockers or they will hate you; rebuke the wise man and they will love you." Who among us loves being rebuked? What a crazy question! Who would invite admonishment? Proverbs says that "the wise" do this.

Practicing real presence before others. Jane next door e-mails me instead of stepping into my room. Derek texts his friend, though his friend is just thirty feet away. I call instead of walk over to a colleague down the hall. In an age that favors second-hand presence, I suggest that we lean toward firsthand presence, that we make the extra effort to be face-to-face whenever we can. "But e-mail is more efficient," we say. Indeed. Firsthand human interaction, true communion, is messier and slower. So what? What's the rush?

One way to make a commitment to firsthand presence is, literally, to count the number of human senses available in our communication—and "lean toward" the choice with the higher number. Face-to-face has the potential to include all five. A video phone call loses touch. A regular phone call loses sight. Voicemail loses hearing. E-mail and texting lose tone of voice. For all its benefits, e-mail's implicit bluntness has been the cause of untold confusion and conflict. Real presence understands that we are sensory creatures. The likelihood of misunderstanding grows exponentially with each sense lost.

Living genuinely before others inevitably requires the spiritual work of confession. Jesus says, "How can you say, . . . 'Let me take the speck out of your eye,' when all the time there is a plank in your own eye? You hypocrite, first take the plank out of your own eye, and then you will see clearly to remove the speck from the other person's eye" (Matthew 7:4-5). As we admit immoral or unwise decisions, we come clean inside and out. When we "come clean" in confession, we also "become clean." We are liberated *esse quam videri*, "to be, rather than to appear to be." By God's grace, we wash away the dirt that keeps us from being real with others—and we feel revitalized.

Confession also calls for courage. We have to trust someone to listen well and to be responsive with forgiveness and encouragement. It's a significant risk. But the alternative is also perilous: to keep our failings buried inside, where they can eat away at our soul. Better to put them on the table before God and a friend.

In our culture, being authentic is both a mystery and a challenge. Part of what gives us the courage to practice an inside-out consistency is the knowledge that Jesus already knows what is on the inside. He knows what we are made of and who we are becoming—and he has chosen to walk beside us anyway. We can imitate his integrity, his sincerity, his genuineness. *Esse quam videri*.

FOR DISCUSSION OR REFLECTION

1. When does the phoniness of our culture or of others' choices most irritate you?

2. What fakery in yourself most troubles you?

3. What do you think about Jesus' authenticity (in Matthew 23 and elsewhere)? Does it attract you? Does it seem at times insensitive? Do you wish you could be more like him in these ways, or do you think his kind of straightforwardness is for the Son of God and not for Jesus-followers?

4. Consider the definition of authenticity in its different compo-

nents (inside-out, rigorous, courageous care for others). Which parts do you struggle most to fulfill and find easiest to fulfill? Walk through a particular experience that yielded mixed results.

5. What evidence do you see that, in keeping with the gospel of sight, you prefer illusion? Consider your definitions of beauty, wealth, popularity and success.

6. Have you ever had an image-consciousness fairy in your life? Discuss experiences you have had being accountable to others for how you present yourself.

EXERCISE

As suggested in the section on real presence before God, take a psalm and create your own fulfillments in the blanks in a genuine way. Try Psalm 6, 51, 84 or 102. For example, write personalized versions of the following verses from Psalm 102:

102:1: Hear my prayer, LORD; let my cry for help come to you.

102:4-5: My heart is blighted and withered like grass; I forget to eat my food. In my distress, I groan aloud and am reduced to skin and bones.

102:19-20: The LORD looked down from his sanctuary on high, from heaven he viewed the earth, to hear the groans of the prisoners and release those condemned to death.

102:23: In the course of my life [the LORD] broke my strength; he cut short my days.

102:27: But you, [O God], remain the same, and your years will never end.

5 ❧ MODESTY

it's not a modest virtue

Mma Ramotswe . . . admired the king of Lesotho, because
he . . . had been a good, wise man (and modest too—
had he not described himself as a flea in the blanket of
Queen Victoria?).

ALEXANDER McCALL SMITH

I still feel awkward shopping with my wife in the lingerie area in a department store. I know we live in carefree times and I shouldn't have any of this pesky sexual shame, but I do. I can't help thinking that I don't belong in aisle after aisle of women's underwear—or that if anyone catches me looking intently, they'll think I'm a degenerate. And it's not that I don't like lingerie or, God knows only too well, the female form.

Sometimes I feel like the last person in America struggling with modesty issues. Of course, this is just more of my immodesty, as if I am so special. But the feeling *does* reflect how embarrassed we are to talk about it, fearing a judgmental sneer. Who wants to be called "not mature enough" to tolerate a crude joke?

When we do engage in conversations about modesty, we often disagree about specifics. What about see-through pants? Exaggerating about our kids in a Christmas letter? Boasting that God told you you'd invent a better parking lot someday? I don't mind a good debate. It's better than concluding that modesty is irrelevant or sexist or that we have, in weariness, given up protecting it or that we just want to avoid conflict.

We need to have this discussion. As I look around at the way we flaunt our bodies, our identities, our nationalism and our faith, the prophet Jeremiah's words ring true: we "do not even know how to blush" (6:15). In fact, we could say that one goal of our culture is to obliterate blushing altogether. So, before I examine modesty, I will address issues of immodesty. Its primary orientation is a self-centered assertion of power: "Look at me!" And its primary defense is that the modest person has the problem and should "Get over it!"

THE IMMODESTY OF "LOOK AT ME!"

A little girl inches her toes across the edge of a curb and flexes her knees for the jump, shouting to her parents, "Look at me!" They attempt to tune out this phrase they've heard dozens of times this morning alone. Then guilt swoops in. They don't want their child to feel unappreciated, so they say, "Okay, we're looking." The girl jumps, displaying no special talent or technique. Her parents shout back, "Great job, honey!"

This innocuous scene is instructive about immodesty. Desiring parental approval, toddlers demand to be noticed. The behavior is charming and natural and not usually to be criticized. Unless it keeps up. Ten, twenty times in a row. Or, obnoxiously, into adulthood. The soul of immodesty is an insecure "look at me" that gets expressed in overstated acts of power that tend to make mounting tensions mount even more.

"Look at me" as boastfulness. Immodesty is most obvious in the irrepressible braggart. Some athletes act as if every score etches their name on some intergalactic trophy. Some adventurers man-

age always to be the hero of their own stories ("The raft would have flipped in the rapids if I hadn't grabbed an oar and pushed us away from the rock"). Then there are those who can connect anything anyone says to their own experience. When you say about your visit to China, "Wait till you hear what a klutz I was on the Great Wall," you are interrupted with, "Wow, that's just like the time I tripped on a glob of gum stuck to a nickel."

The tragedy of David and Bathsheba can teach us something about the way "look at me" is often an abuse of power. As beautiful Bathsheba bathed in a place that could be seen from a rooftop, David watched her. He was so taken by her beauty that he "sent messengers to get her. She came to him, and he slept with her" (2 Samuel 11:4). In essence, he said to her, "I am king, so I can break God's rules about adultery." David's use of power was immodest; his overstated self-importance gave him the courage to act on his lust. Only when his choices included the murder of Bathsheba's husband (another form of immodesty) did David see his folly. David's power inflated his sense of importance, and he needed to repent of his arrogant choices.

We can read this story and feel good about our own choices. After all, *we* are not going to have sex with a sunbather next door and then murder the spouse! But we shouldn't miss the immodesty we have in common with David. We often exaggerate our deservedness or assert our will with too much confidence: "I'm so smart, I ought to be respected." "I earned my wealth; I have a right to go ahead of others."

Philosopher Joseph Kupfer says that the arrogant person falsely perceives "that other people owe him deference since he is entitled to disregard their interests in favor of his own." If you aren't sure of your Boastfulness Quotient, ask yourself a few questions: Do I consistently draw attention to myself in conversations? Do I often judge others for not measuring up? Do I think that others spend a lot of time evaluating my actions? Do I attempt to elicit praise to shore up my insecurities? Modesty tempers these forms of boast-fulness because it is more concerned with the *stewardship* of power than with the *assertion* of power.

Early in our marriage, my wife, Janet, stumbled onto an important revelation regarding the power of my verbal confidence. After I stated my opinion about something—in my estimation, present-ing it tentatively—Janet paused and said, "You don't know what you are talking about, do you?"

I said, "No, not really."

Louder, she said, "You truly don't know what you are talking about!"

"No, I'm not sure," I said. "I'm just stating my opinion at this point."

She threw up her hands. "Then why do you *sound* like you know what you are talking about?!"

Immodesty's "look at me" arrogance often shows up in conver-sation. Have you had the following experience? After talking with friends you haven't seen in a while, even after hours and hours together, you realize they have no new knowledge of you except for what you volunteered, because they haven't asked you a *single* question. Harold Barrett points to the way out: Success in com-munication "entails looking outside the self. . . . Those who see only themselves in others find only themselves—and talk only to themselves." Good conversation is other-centered, a commitment that immodest narcissists find difficult to live by.

"Look at me" as escalation-enhancer. Years ago, when standing in line in a post office, I noticed an attractive woman ahead of me. She noticed me too and—in a glance—seemed to say, "I'm yours." I might have been flattering myself (nothing new there!), but the experience shows how immodesty arouses. It says "look at me and, if you would, please imagine what might happen next." Mag-azine covers announce, "Sexy in Sixty Seconds!" or "Twenty-Seven New Ways to Please Her in Bed." In our times, we are so focused

on maximizing the escalation of sexual tensions that our priorities are often unconscionable. We care more about the latest catchy song than we do about poverty, more about beautiful hair than about global disease. Our contemporary secular doctrine is that looking sexy is the key to human happiness.

Immodesty certainly relates to sexual dynamics, but it can also exacerbate all conflicts involving power, from friendly disagreements to military combat. When swaggering doesn't keep others intimidated and therefore submissive, it can raise the stakes, which leads our foes to raise the stakes higher, which leads to more strutting and swaggering. It's called war. Petty disagreements over the rules of golf have led to murder. Perceptions of freeway rudeness have justified turning cars into weapons. Such is the fruit of the tree of immodesty.

When some friends of mine married, they discovered that—since both were raised without siblings—they tended to act like a king and a queen. "But the problem was," they said, "we didn't have any servants." Immodesty's "look at me" insists on royal deference. Inevitably, it asks others to function as hired help.

THE IMMODESTY OF "GET OVER IT!"

When my parents wanted me to clean my room, my response was the classic line of many teenagers: "Get over it." The argument goes like this: "The problem you have with my behavior is really *your* problem. There's nothing wrong with trash and wet towels on the floor. You are too uptight. Get over it." Sometimes this argument is appropriate because the issue in contention is just a matter of convention, of taste. As the saying goes, "Don't sweat the small stuff." But not everything is small stuff.

"Get over it" as "More now is always better." The idea is that *you* should get over it because it's *your* modesty that's keeping me from grabbing all that I can. The less modest we are, the more we will gain. Sexual modesty is out-of-date, stuck in some stuffy Victorian reti-

cence about the horrors of exposing a woman's ankle. Ego modesty is akin to self-loathing, and national modesty is downright unpatriotic.

There's some truth here. People *can* be too self-effacing. A friend of mine once signed a letter not "Brian," but "A nobody," thereby immodestly drawing attention to his humility. But the defenders of go-for-it-now immodesty often miss how short-sighted this sentiment is. Flaunting one's body may turn some heads at seventeen, but it won't necessarily attract people who turn out to be good spouses. The tough guy who prides himself on never backing down might later discover that he has a hard time keeping a job. Modesty takes on a long-term view: not *this present* flirtatious thrill, but *that future* secure marriage, not *this* perfect put-down, but *that* enduring friendship.

"Get over it" as absolute free choice. The idea here is that *you* should get over it because *your* modesty is keeping me from the limitless autonomy that is my birthright. We all know the story. A young man leaves home to be free to do what he wants, but he squanders his opportunities and ends up a drunk. Immodesty's insistence on freedom can justify gross wastefulness, just as it did for the prodigal son. This do-as-I-please immodesty doesn't care how many water bottles get piled into a landfill or who suffers for the sake of personal advancement. Sometimes this kind of freedom ends up where the prodigal son did, in a pig trough. Yet no matter how many times the story is told about the "road to ruin," we think we would be the exception. We would use the immodesty of absolute freedom to find success. The prodigal son had his plans too.

The problem isn't freedom but our practice of it. Wendell Berry understands our contradictory commitment to free choice:

> To try to draw the line where we are trying to draw it, between carelessness and brutality, is like insisting that falling is flying—until you hit the ground—and then trying to outlaw hitting the ground.

He means that we encourage careless flying (doing whatever we want) when it's not flying at all, but falling (a moral collapse with serious consequences). Then we say that the brutality of hitting the ground is against the law. Our culture says, "Watch porn and be promiscuous, but we'll send you to jail for sexual abuse." It says, "Do whatever it takes to get ahead in business, but we'll prosecute for embezzlement or tax evasion."

Immodesty boasts that wholesale freedom won't lead to disaster. It says, "Don't worry; everything will be fine." But everything won't be fine. Human nature isn't all peaches and teddy bears and sharing our last chunk of chocolate. As Jesus says, "For from within, out of your hearts, come evil thoughts, sexual immorality, theft, murder, adultery, greed, malice, deceit, lewdness, envy, slander, arrogance and folly" (Mark 7:21-22). Absolute free choice doesn't lead to freedom. Unless we restrict our immodesties, we will suffer their effects.

Followers of Jesus have their own ways of manifesting "look at me" and "get over it." Some shine the light on themselves with the way they speak for God, saying, "God told me" as easily as "I want." And the "get over it" Christians flaunt their sense of chosenness, using it to justify their politics of neglect, their hatred for other groups and their arrogant approach to free enterprise.

Is our sense of self in step with Scripture? It certainly isn't in step with traditional Christian literature. Comparing seventeenth-century Christian works with contemporary Christian writing, Kari Konkola says that "power has displaced humility as a core Christian aspiration." While earlier Christians often wrote about the problems of unchecked pride, we are more likely to glorify the influence of a Christian athlete or politician.

Immodesty goes by a host of names, some that hide its flaws (such as liberation, flirtatious fun, "selling yourself") and others that tell it straight (such as compulsion, seduction, arrogance). To many, modesty seems laughable, a weak-minded attitude for prudes too embarrassed to show an inch of skin. By whatever name, unless we feel the wounds immodesty has cut into our world, we will not be interested in pulling back the blade.

A MODEST DEFINITION

A few older terms get us started. The Greek word for modesty, *kosmios*, means "well ordered, decent." The Latin term, *modestus*, means "moderate, keeping within boundaries." Although these behaviors all have their place, they tend to get us thinking in the direction of mild-mannered restraint, as if we should act like Clark Kent in a world of superheroes. Is modesty the same as painstakingly walking a balance beam, worrying every minute about falling off, about leaning too far to the left or the right?

If the ways of Jesus are meant to free us to become our best selves, living adventurously under the canopy of God's love and trustworthiness, modesty should not be posed primarily in negative terms. It certainly includes caution or reserve, but I say that modesty is *gladly tempering the expression of our fullness with an understanding of our emptiness.* Modesty calls us to the joyful act of presenting all that our words and bodies and organizations have to offer—but appropriately, acknowledging our deficiencies.

Understanding our emptiness. Given how difficult it is to be truly good in motive and deed, one wouldn't think we would need to be convinced we are empty and need filling. Such is the irony of our lives. We seem to be the neediest yet most self-satisfied generation of all time.

Many writers take a dim view of human nature. Some of these writers appear in the Bible. Paul says, "Do not think of yourself more highly than you ought, but rather think of yourself with sober judgment, in accordance with the faith God has distributed to each of you" (Romans 12:3). Sober judgment does not sound like a key value in a self-esteem curriculum.

Without a doubt, understanding our emptiness will require humility. George MacDonald writes, "Those who are poor in spirit, who *feel themselves poor creatures*; . . . who know that they need much to make their life worth living, to make their existence a good thing, to make them fit to live; these humble ones are the poor whom the Lord calls blessed." I don't know about you, but I feel knocked over by these words. Too often I do not act as though I "need much" to make my life worth living. Yet until we speak the truth about our emptiness, we will not get on the path to modesty.

One of the great falsehoods of our age is that in our basic state, we are "great." And espousing this lie weighs us down with the burden of presenting ourselves as great, a burden that keeps us from disclosing the ways in which we are deeply greedy or secretly addicted or compulsively angry. Thomas à Kempis put it well: "We are all frail; consider none more frail than yourself."

Fullness and emptiness in our self-image. Maybe you can identify with the following experience. You do something well—win an award or give an insightful word of advice—and receive praise for it. You feel pretty good about yourself and wonder if a line of well-wishers will start to form. You are Really Something. Then, the very next thing you do is make a joke at someone's expense. You feel terrible. You think, "How is it possible that in five minutes I can go from being the best thing since sliced bread to a moldy, stinky muffin? How can I be an Amazingly Fabulous Person *and* the World's Most Disgusting Person?"

The answer is that each title represents the same sentiment: everything revolves around me. Typically, we attach "center of the universe" labels to irritating narcissists, such as our own children between the ages of twelve and nineteen. At the same time, we know that when our teenagers are blowing smoke, the dusky stuff is often caused by a fire of insecurity. And so it is with all of us. When we see the world revolving around us—positively or negatively—we are putting ourselves in the center, a tendency that could also be called "preoccupation with the self." The continuum in figure 1 captures various ways we express this self-centered-ness, from the extreme negative of self-loathing to the extreme positive of self-worship.

PREOCCUPATION WITH THE SELF

NEG					POS
self-loathing	self-pity	self-deprecation	self-meekness	self-praise	self-worship
I hate myself.	*Woe is me.*	*I'm such a jerk.*	*It was nothing.*	*I'm terrific!*	*Adore me!*

Figure 1.

We often hear that the way to stop hating ourselves is to start loving ourselves, that we should stop saying "Woe is me!" to ourselves and start saying "I'm terrific!" Yet this change just moves us from left to right on the same continuum—when the better goal is to get off the continuum altogether. Being preoccupied with ourselves positively may *feel* better than being preoccupied negatively, but it is no less self-centered.

Of course, not only are we *not* the center of the universe, we aren't the center of the nation, the city, the neighborhood or even our own house. We aren't usually the center of *anyone's* attention because everyone else is the center of his or her own world. As my friend David Downing learned from his mother, "You'd worry less about what others think of you if you realized how seldom they do."

Modesty is made more difficult by our culture's teaching about the self. We fill our children exclusively with praise and then are surprised they are smug. And we've twisted Jesus' words about the most important commandments. He said there are two (to love God and our neighbor as ourselves: Mark 12:29-31), but we say there are three, to love ourselves also.

Some people reason that we can't love our neighbors as ourselves unless we first love ourselves. But Jesus says there are only two commandments ("the *second* is this")—and the assumption he makes is that we naturally love ourselves. When we are hungry, we seek food. When a truck rushes toward us, we get out of the way. In fact, Paul says that one of the signs of the terrible last days is that "people will be lovers of themselves" (2 Timothy 3:2).

"But," you may ask, "does modesty mean that we should hate ourselves, that we should hang our head wherever we go?" Absolutely not. Remember the continuum. Self-pity is no better than self-praise. As Jeremy Taylor said in the mid-seventeenth century, "Humility does not consist in criticizing yourself, or wearing ragged clothes, or walking around submissively wherever you go. Humility consists in a realistic opinion of yourself, namely that you are an unworthy person." For Taylor, humility (the inward life of modesty) is not about hating or loving ourselves; it is about knowing we are needy people and responding to God for help with that need.

"But," you may ask, "should we never think of ourselves positively?" Of course we should. However, our goal, contrary to cultural ideals, is not to have a positive self-image but, as Taylor clearly saw, an accurate one. Our *sense* of fullness or emptiness is not the same thing as our true fullness or emptiness. Arrogant folks can feel full even though many observers see their emptiness. Oppressed folks slump over even though their friends can list a dozen of their wonderful qualities. The question before us is, Am I willing and able to see myself as I really am—as God sees me?

Modesty means that we hold on to a duality. We temper the fullness of our belovedness in the eyes of God with our need for grace, our state of inadequacy before the standards of a genuinely holy life. We are loved, but not because of our righteous deservedness. Paul captures the paradox: "But by the grace of God I am what I am, and his grace to me was not without effect" (1 Corinthians 15:10).

Gladly tempering how we express ourselves. Modesty lives in the joy of knowing that though we might have been condemned for our thoughts and actions, we have instead been saved. Modesty is the skip in our step that comes from realizing that though we have the power to manipulate others and demand that they conform to our will, we don't have to. We can move aside; we can endure not being noticed. Our security is in Christ, not in getting others to flatter us.

Modesty gives us the strength to be careful caretakers of our personal power—and in this way modesty reveals itself as a child of temperance, the virtue that would have us thinking about the appropriateness of our actions. Temperance does not mean that we are always to be moderate, as if modesty would keep us from doing something with all our hearts. Sometimes being appropriate means shouting at an intruder to get away or asserting truth in a hostile environment or screaming for joy at seeing a long-lost friend. We are not immodest when we appropriately discipline our children in public or divulge an intimate transgression for the sake of empathizing with a friend.

So, a glad tempering of the expression of our fullness tells us that being modest is not the same thing as being prudish. Modesty is born out of a confidence in God's love for us, not a worry that every immodest act will lead to the collapse of society. Though the modest person will, at times, make the same outward choices as the prudish person, the inner attitude is quite different. The prude is snobbish and governed by fear. The modest person is welcoming and affirming, whenever possible. The prude says, "No, you don't belong; you are beneath me." The modest person says, "Yes, I too have those desires—but I am trying to learn a better way." True modesty is not off-putting; it is inviting. That's why Jesus could be "a friend of tax collectors and sinners" (Matthew 11:19).

Also, a glad tempering of the expression of our fullness tells us that being modest is not the same thing as being painfully meek. Many today confuse modesty with passivity. They think that being a good Christian means being nice, not causing a scene, never interfering with the general flow of pleasantries. But modesty is not the fear of getting attention, as if no modest person could ever occupy a stage or a pulpit or put her or his name on a book(!). It is not "I should never be dramatic, because that would be showing off." Some are called to be leaders and speakers. All of us, at times, are called to proclaim, protest or even admonish.

Though modesty is not always in the back seat, it does its best to drive considerately. Although "niceness" is overstated in the church, kindness and gentleness are understated. Ironically, outsiders often see Christians as feisty, intolerant and arrogant, the exact opposite of the Christians in the niceness group. Modesty moves mousy types into a glad expression of their fullness, but it also moves obstinate types toward a gentleness that takes their own emptiness into consideration.

THE BODY OF MODESTY: HEART, TONGUE, APPEARANCE AND TOUCH

Modesty is not a modest virtue. We might think it is limited to how much skin we show, but modesty inhabits a whole body of application. It pertains to the fullness and emptiness living in our motives, speech, appearance and touch.

Modesty of motive. In the Sermon on the Mount, Jesus names anger and lust as the heart of murder and adultery, and he discourages attention-grabbing tithing, boastful prayer and flagrant fasting. Heart sentiments matter. Our motives are part of our modesty.

One test of heart modesty compares personal assessments with conclusions reached by others. Taylor says, "When you hold [a humble, modest] opinion of yourself, be content that others think the same of you. If you realize that you are not wise, do not be angry if someone else should agree!" When I say I am a lousy bowler and others agree with me, I simply laugh at my own bowling ineptitude. I can do this because I do not care about my image as a poor bowler. But if I say that I'm not sure if a chapter I am writing is hitting the mark, and a reader agrees, I can feel hurt. My personal modesty is not fully modesty of the heart until my pride is not offended when others criticize me.

Modesty of speech. Jesus can seem downright odd to us. After he heals a blind man—a great PR opportunity if ever there was one—he commands the guy not to tell anyone (Mark 8:25-26). Most of us can't imagine this level of restraint. It's like the shock I felt when visiting the Netherlands. The locals kept saying, "Holland is a small country. There's not too much to get excited about." American Christians, on the other hand, are all about pride. We're the number-one country in the world and, we believe, the number-one religion. Too many of us go from needing the Messiah to having a messiah complex.

Modesty disciplines our words because it knows the results of not doing so. Proverbs 18:21 says, "The tongue has the power of life and death, and those who love it will eat its fruit." Immodest accusations can lead to defensiveness, gossip to distrust, and ridicule to embarrassment and withdrawal.

Recognizing the power of the tongue, modesty takes a long-term perspective, especially toward weaker members of our society. We have probably all observed the wounds caused by a few reckless statements. It's hard to recover from "you will never amount to anything" or "my coworker is such a whiny kiss-up." Modesty leans toward words that give the other grace, words that don't presume an evil motive. If we say we don't mean any harm, why do we keep picking up all those hammering words?

We are also remarkably free to talk about every detail of our sexual encounters or every suture in our hemorrhoid operation. A cartoon called this the Too Much Information syndrome. Sometimes we are just trying to get noticed in a world with so much noisy competition. By contrast, a disciplined tongue inspires confidentiality. When I know you will not pass along what you hear or embellish stories, I know you can be trusted.

Modesty of appearance. "You are not going out in public wearing *that!*" When our three daughters were in high school, my wife and I had our share of clothing-related debates. Though their choices were often perfectly acceptable, they defended their questionable fashions by saying, "everybody dresses like this" or "there are no stylish options" or "boys don't look at us anyway." Right.

These issues aren't new. In a college meeting my wife attended, a speaker addressed the importance of modest appearance. The discussion revealed great resonance among the students. Later during refreshments, Janet saw about five guys standing around the most scantily clad female there. She despaired. Can we really say we are committed to the sexual health of our community when we wear seductive clothing that seems to say, "Look here! Don't pass this up"?

Appearance is such a confounding issue because dress is not the only factor, or even the most important factor, in sexual presentation. "I am sexually available to you" is the message that messes with a commitment to modesty—and, of course, sexual availability can be communicated in a polka-dot bikini or an Alaskan parka. Two important questions can help us to navigate these difficult waters. First, do I intend to make a sexually immodest statement with my appearance? The defense that "I had no idea" is not usually convincing. Second, what do others say about my appearance? If, in some cases, community values have higher priority over personal expression, we should be willing to find friends who would give us their opinion.

Modesty of touch. More tricky territory. I don't want to give you a list of what you shouldn't wear any more than I want to prescribe quantifiable rules about how you shouldn't touch. It's not my job; it's yours. And, as with most of what we do, touch depends on context. A deep hug can mean "I feel terrible about what has happened to you," and one finger on an arm can mean "I am flirting with all of my being," and so on.

Men and women can be amazingly foolish or falsely naive about the power of touch. Once, in my office, a female student seated across from me touched my knee as she talked. I shuffled my chair back and she shuffled forward, pressing her point on my knee again and again. Soon, I was against the wall. Did she not know that such a gesture could feel like a sexual statement? Or did she know and touch anyway? Irrespective of her motive, the gesture was inappropriate, as is most sexually charged touch on the job or between neighbors. Too often we drive through life like maniacs and then act surprised when we crash. But what could I say to my student? If I told her I was uncomfortable with her gestures, she could accuse me of sexual harassment, of interpreting her innocent touch as sexual in nature. And this is where we are these days—overly tolerant of sexual activity and therefore sexually oppressed—which brings me to my next point.

Our culture has so eroticized human contact that we tend to see all touch as sexual, a stance that actually results in *less* physical affection. We say, "Here is a body on display. You may gaze on it and think of it in sexual terms. Do whatever you can to touch it." Then we say, "Don't touch! Why are you being so sexual?" Fearing that our touch will be misinterpreted, we abstain.

Perhaps we have sexualized touch *because* we touch so little. As communication with phones and computers increases, direct human contact decreases—yet we suffer from this loss of touch. Perhaps this explains the physical metaphors we use for technology. In e-mails, we say, "Stay in touch." Phone companies say, "Make connections." Movie reviews say, "Feel the heat." Because we touch each other less, we pretend that not touching is, in fact, touching.

Paradoxes abound. We touch too much. We touch too little. Modesty helps us resolve this conundrum because, if practiced well, modesty allows us to touch more freely. Knowing our emptiness, we are able to express our fullness.

Modesty is not a modest virtue. It makes a difference in the way we think, talk, dress and touch. As such a large virtue, it requires a large discipline.

✿ THE DISCIPLINE OF TIMELY REMEMBRANCE

In *The Giver*, Lois Lowry tells the story of how a society becomes bland and controlled when everyone except one person is disconnected from the past. After the main character, Jonas, is chosen as the community's next memory holder, or Receiver, he learns that remembering is important because that's "how wisdom comes. And how we shape our future."

For those interested in fostering modesty, "timely remembrance" is the key discipline. Wisdom comes from spiritual self-examination, especially when we reflect on excessive pride. Too many of us practice intentional amnesia, forgetting our immodesties as soon as possible so that we can "move on." On the other hand, some never forget, punishing themselves relentlessly. Instead of choosing amnesia, we need to practice a godly *anamnesis*, the act of resisting forgetfulness. In *The Living Reminder*, Henri Nouwen says, "Forgetting the past is like turning our most intimate teacher against us. . . . Only those who face their wounded condition can be available for healing and so enter into a new way of living."

Timely remembrance has a lot to offer, and I think its richness is found in Jesus' Last Supper: "And he took bread, gave thanks and broke it, and gave it to them, saying, 'This is my body given for you; do this in remembrance of me'" (Luke 22:19). Using Jesus' words and Henri Nouwen's commentary for inspiration, I would like to offer a meditation on the importance of remembering for the sake of modesty. Here are the basics: Jesus took the bread, gave thanks, broke it and gave it to his disciples.

Taking the timely remembrance: Recollect in truth. Jesus took the bread and said, "This is my body." Although the disciples did not want to hear it, Jesus told them the hard truth that he was going to die. Likewise, in timely remembrance, we take the time to recount the truth about an experience. As best we can, we are not to make ourselves look better than we were—or worse. Our tendency to change our memories over time, usually in a way that justifies our actions, is one of the reasons our remembrance needs to be timely, before we lose the knowledge that might lead to greater modesty. Even when we have been wronged—especially when we have been wronged—we should strive to remember well, asking others for their impressions, knowing that along the way, we may learn about our own mistakes and need to suffer modesty. "Taking the timely remembrance" is not a nostalgic move, a sweet sentimentalizing of the past. It is a humble and brave recollection.

Giving thanks for the timely remembrance: Recollect in prayer. Without gratitude for what God might teach us, we might not proceed at all. Without a sense that God is there to catch us, we might not risk the leap into timely remembrance. So, as Jesus did, we pray gratefully. We ask that our self-examination would teach us who we are before God, would lead us to an accurate self-image. As St. Augustine said, "I beg you, my God, to reveal me to my own eyes." Admitting our neediness is crucial for the growth of modesty, because our fullness requires an understanding of our emptiness.

Being broken by the timely remembrance: Recollect in openness. The hardest part is letting the remembrance do its work in us by sweating through the labor of self-examination so we might be changed by the Holy Spirit. For memory to be our teacher, we have to be its student. As difficult as it is to drop our defensiveness, we can come to the task in hope, because we know that Jesus' body was broken for us, and redemption was the result. We must ask ourselves: "Was I immodest in motive, speech, appearance or touch? Did I love my neighbor as myself?"

Sometimes we underplay our flaws and overplay the harm done

to us. Sometimes we do the opposite, multiplying our shame, piling on the pounds till we are obese with remorse. If we submit to modesty well, we may say with the psalmist, "My sacrifice, O God, is a broken spirit" (Psalm 51:17).

Giving the timely remembrance: Recollect in community. In the Lord's Supper, the bread is broken and then it is given. In timely remembrance, this means sharing our reflections for the sake of others. We must be careful here, because nothing defeats modesty faster than becoming proud of it. So, our gift to the community is not a story about the growth of our modesty ("I was so humbled"), but a report about what we learned, a task that requires modesty to share ("I have a problem with pride").

Here's an example of how this practice of timely remembrance has led to greater modesty. After ten years of marriage, Trisha decided she couldn't take the verbal abuse anymore. Karl seemed to be angry about everything: her incompetence with practical things, her inadequate reasoning, her messes on the dresser. So Trisha told Karl that she felt consistently demeaned by his impatience and embarrassed by his public criticism. Initially, Karl felt the sting to his pride. He resisted, saying, "You're overreacting. I care about you."

But Trisha pressed the issue, and Karl reluctantly entertained the possibility that she was right, or partially right. Yet even this faltering acceptance was a good first step, a taking in of the truth. By receiving it, he could work toward a more accurate self-image. Next, he prayed. He asked to be made willing to be humbled—not blindly, but with good discernment. He asked God to bless the timely remembrance.

More evidence from Trisha arrived: the time he called her stupid, the way he dismissed her vocation and her contributions to the home. Karl groaned under the weight, and he was broken in this openness. He saw that this "not him" was really a part of him. He made a more modest assessment of what he brought to the marriage. Karl reflected on his claim that he cared about her—and he still believed this—but now he saw how his anger diminished Trisha, how it allowed him to get his way at her expense.

In time, Karl's increased modesty allowed him to give the benefit of this remembrance back to the community. He communicated to friends about his failures and about God's help in overcoming them. He slowly changed his life. Recognizing a pattern of anger with others besides Trisha, he sought their forgiveness. Eventually, friends sought him out for advice in their own marriages.

We live in a community of memory, the church. We remember God, and we ask him to remember us. We remind him of his promises, and we remind ourselves of what it means to follow him. When these memories reveal to us how far we have to go in imitation of him, we tell the truth, ask for help, allow ourselves to be broken for his sake, and then we return the experience back to the church for the sake of God. We learn modesty in remembrance of him.

It turns out that modesty is not a modest virtue. Since it reaches into our heart, speech, appearance and touch, its expansiveness and importance is worth our attention. Gladly tempering the expression of our fullness with an understanding of our emptiness is a large task, particularly in a culture that constantly tells us how wonderful we are, even while it exposes our imperfections. So, we have a lot of work to do resisting the wrong messages and persisting in the right messages. Thank God we are not alone in this task.

FOR DISCUSSION OR REFLECTION

1. The word *modesty* tends to be weighed down with considerable baggage. What associations with this word stand in the way of desiring it as a virtue?

2. What cultural immodesties bother you? What immodesties seem to bother others but not you?

3. Where is modesty a strength or a struggle for you? About what sorts of things do you tend to say "look at me" or "get over it"?

4. Jesus said, "No one comes to the Father except through me," "Get behind me, Satan," and "Today you will be with me in paradise." No humble pie here. So, was Jesus immodest—or is the question moot because Jesus was the Son of God and can say whatever he wants? How could you support the idea that Jesus was, in fact, modest?

5. Aleksandr Solzhenitsyn said that the problem in our times pertains not so much to the "right to know" as it does to "the forfeited right of people *not to know*, not to have their divine souls stuffed with gossip, nonsense, vain talk." When do you encounter invasive or seductive immodesties?

6. Modesty is gladly tempering the expression of our fullness with an understanding of our emptiness. What examples of modesty can you cite that fulfill this definition? What areas of the definition do you resist?

7. As you consider modesty as applied to heart, speech, appearance and touch, recount experiences where modesty made a positive difference. When are you usually modest in these areas—and usually not?

EXERCISE

1. In a journal, write about a time you were immodest or when your immodesty was exposed and you felt embarrassment or regret. As described in the section on timely remembrance, recollect in truth, in prayer and in openness.

2. With a friend or in a group, recollect in community, sharing your experience for the benefit of others.

6 ❧ REVERENCE

the church without shoes

You are my God, my Life, my holy Delight, but is this enough to say of you? Can any man say enough when he speaks of you?

ST. AUGUSTINE

At a worship service recently, when people in the congregation were told they were about to enter into the presence of deity, they audibly gasped. The glorious expressions on these worshipers' faces revealed their deep longing for the supernatural, for something sacred and transcendent.

Then it happened.

The holy one descended—and the congregation erupted into screams of spontaneous joy. Yes, the object of adoration, the Handsomest Man Alive, walked in, said hello to the talk-show host and sat down. As women in the audience swooned, the actor signed a prop from a movie and gave it to a venerating soul trembling before him.

Such reverence! When I hear the word, I remember my days as a Boy Scout, when I pledged to be "brave, clean and reverent." Sounds quaint, no? Yet good reverence is still with us. Worship music and worship ministers—more than in decades past—seem to call up a sense of awe and deference. At the same time, contemporary worship can feel like a show, too relentlessly upbeat to feel genuinely connected to the holy.

In general culture, when we aren't revering celebrities and rock stars, we are going in the opposite direction, applauding stories of their disrespectful or morally shocking qualities. Movie critics say, "Go see this film. It's sassy and irreverent." We enjoy seeing the powerful knocked down. We also seem to be less and less awed by what we observe—or, at least, we don't direct our sense of wonder to much of anything beyond the latest technological innovation. Ceremony is often ridiculed; traditions are diminished. Has our recognition of "the sacred" actually faded, or are we just searching for transcendence in different, more secular places?

WHAT A PLANT ON FIRE HAS TO DO WITH GOING BAREFOOT

Moses understood something about reverence, but he needed help to get there. While tending the flock of his father-in-law, Jethro, Moses encountered a freakishly burning bush. As he got closer, he heard, "Take off your sandals, for the place where you are standing is holy ground" (Exodus 3:5). Such an odd statement. What makes ground holy? And why didn't Moses recognize the presence of holiness? Why is taking off one's shoes (near fire!) the appropriate response? Is it that our shoes carry the dust of the world? Is it that we need to be more vulnerable, more fleshy, so we can feel what is underneath, the ground of God's being?

Based on this passage featuring Moses, we might see reverence as "taking off our shoes in the presence of holiness." That's not a bad start. It speaks to the protective coverings we need to remove in order to expose our vulnerabilities: the sandals called accomplishments, the dress shoes of status or position. But perhaps this Moses orientation doesn't tell us quite enough about reverence.

REVERENCE THAT ATTENDS TO SHOES AND KNEES

Whatever reverence looks like, it is not pious performance. It is not about seeking affirmation with pleading hands or sweet public prayers. Jesus is tough on public reverence: "When you fast, do not look somber as the hypocrites do, for they disfigure their faces to show others they are fasting. Truly I tell you, they have received their reward in full" (Matthew 6:16). Reverence does not draw attention to itself by showing off or by being so stick-in-the-mud serious that others think we are being punished.

Lawrence H. Davis says that reverence is "a rational response to awareness of God's exaltedness." Paul Woodruff says it is "the well-developed capacity to have feelings of awe, respect, and shame when they are the right feelings to have." Whereas Davis emphasizes the importance of ways we think about the object of reverence, God, Woodruff highlights emotion and the experience of being reverent. To me, reverence combines all of the above. It is, *in faith, kneeling before the sacred and standing up to the profane.*

I live among people with calloused knees. Prayer warriors? No, surfers. They've knelt on their boards so often they've toughened up their knees. Some have gnarly knobs that look like volcanic malignant tumors, and I mean that in the most complimentary way. I'm impressed with surfers because kneeling hurts, yet they gladly endure the pain because of the glory they trust they'll experience. And that's really how they talk, as if riding a wave is spiritual. Like surfers, we need to know how to kneel and how to stand up.

Kneeling before the sacred. The reverent among us possess excellent vision. They have trained themselves to see God's Spirit and his handiwork. They know the sacred when they see it, and the sacred is that in which God is found. With a finely tuned lens, there is much to see. Typically, we connect the sacred with holiness, righteousness, purity—and these are good associations—but we shouldn't miss other aspects of the sacred: God's love, light, meaning and goodness, the genius of human genomes, the beauty of an owl's whispering flight, the privilege of practicing mercy. Noticing the sacred is noticing all of God that we can see, especially his holiness. Sometimes the sacred is found because it is searched for. Sometimes it seems to crash upon us unannounced. Either way, reverence increases as we cultivate eyes and ears for the God who is there.

And what do we do when we see a burning bush? One way or another, we show our deference to Someone Greater. In four different stories in Matthew, people seek Jesus' healing power by kneeling before him (8:2; 9:18; 15:25; 17:14). Both Jesus and Paul kneel in prayer (Luke 22:41; Acts 20:36). In Revelation, the New Testament book with perhaps the most references to worship, the angels, the elders and the four living creatures all fall down before the throne of God (Revelation 5:8; 7:11; 19:4).

Standing up to the profane. Such a nasty word, *profane.* It conjures up hateful little devils hissing curses or an arrogant Bible-banger blathering on about a blasphemous cartoon character. But if we care for the sacred, we care about what tears it down. *Profane* sounds ugly, as it should. The profane is that which intentionally dismisses, ridicules or destroys the sacred. When our loved ones are attacked or defiled, don't we bristle and seek to defend them? Aren't we saddened when they are misrepresented, ostracized or harmed? And so it is in our life with the Lover of our souls. Who cares about sacrilege these days? The reverent do.

Bob Pierce, the founder of World Vision, famously said, "Let my heart be broken by the things that break the heart of God." Though Pierce was referring to a compassionate response to hunger, I believe the application works well in relationship to the profane. Standing up to the profane means that we notice what breaks the heart of God and that we resist it. To put it another way, a nose for the profane sniffs out what smells to high heaven.

Of course, not everything that stinks to us is offensive to God. If the sacred is not violated in a way that grieves God, the situation is not profane. Who is more profane, an actress who claims to be "doing the Lord's work" by portraying a seductress in her sin or a TV preacher who sells "holy fabric" so viewers can touch it and be healed? Is hunger in a wealthy country profane? What about flaunting a recent theft or allowing a defenseless person to be abused? And how we stand up to the profane matters. We should not put a tag on our chest that says, "God's prophet for accusing others of ungodly acts." The irony is just too obvious.

THE REVERENCE CONTINUUM

Back to surfers for a minute. All forms of good reverence, even trusting a wave, are expressions of faith, reverence's parent virtue. Is God good? Will he carry us to the shore? How should we life-riders regard him? Reverence recognizes that the most appropriate response to the sacred is to kneel before it, and the most appropriate response to what destroys the sacred is to stand up to it. As I see it, reverence gets expressed in a kind of progression from fear to joy.

Fear → Shame → Awe → Respect → Gratitude → Joy

It's not hard to picture someone kneeling in a way that reflects each different aspect of the continuum, from a fearful criminal begging for mercy to a joyful daughter hearing that her mother's tumor is benign. That's one point I want to make: all six responses are appropriate in certain circumstances. Another way to think about the continuum is to see that the preferred movement is from left to right. In other words, though fear is at times the most fittingly reverent response to God, we should—on the whole—be expressing our reverence more and more in terms of gratitude and joy.

Reverence as fear. As I began graduate school, I was asked to take an exam to assess the strengths and weaknesses of my knowledge. When discussing one of my answers, a professor said disdainfully, "Greg, I thought your comments were interesting, and

I'm being kind." I was devastated. In that moment, I felt all my bones turn to mush, and I nearly slid off the chair into a puddle on the floor. Not surprisingly, for quite some time, I had a palpable fear of this professor.

When most of us think about fear in relationship to God, we usually consider the non-bone-melting qualities of awe or respect. Though I'll get to these two areas a bit later, I'll restrict the discussion here to genuine, afraid-of fear or I'm-falling-off-a-cliff-and-I'm-going-to-die fear. This is the fear we fear to discuss. We don't really believe "being afraid" has any place in a Jesus-follower's life because Jesus is a really nice guy and our buddy. We forget that, as Dan Allender and Tremper Longman put it, "exclusive emphasis on these truths about God robs us of the comfort of knowing that God is also . . . the Judge who determines who lives and who dies. . . . He is a being so far above us that we cannot even fathom him."

I don't know about you, but Jesus scares me with his warning about how he'll separate the sheep and goats and send the goats, who did not attend to "the least" among us, to eternal punishment (Matthew 25:31-46). He said this not long after he cursed a fig tree because it did not bear fruit—and the tree withered and died (21:18-19). Jesus may be the son of love, but he is also the one who told Peter, "Get behind me, Satan!" (Mark 8:33). Would it be appropriate to stroll up to God and say, "Hey Big Guy, nice job on the giraffe"?

Reverence requires good fear when nothing else motivates us. Proverbs 9:10 says, "The fear of the LORD is the beginning of wisdom, and knowledge of the Holy One is understanding." Sometimes the only thing that gets us started in the right direction is fear: the fear of getting caught or the fear of being embarrassed at poor performance. Fear may not be the *end* of wisdom, but it is often the *beginning* because it shows we recognize our impoverishment. If fear is the only thing that gets us to kneel, then being frightened by God's power and holiness is meaningful, though being in this situation might reveal more about us than it does about God. Fear can be God's alarm clock for those who aren't sufficiently awake.

When my daughter Emily was two, she loved our wood stove—to a fault. No matter how many times we warned her, she reached for its intensely hot metal. One evening when we weren't watching, she touched it. We felt terrible that it burned her, but she needed fear to motivate her to do the right thing.

Good fear can also put bad fear in its place. If we worship the gods of acceptance, popularity and success, we will overly fear rejection, loneliness and failure. If we revere God more, we will fear these lesser gods less. Whom do we most fear to disappoint?

Reverence as shame. In the presence of holiness, Isaiah said, "Woe to me! . . . I am ruined! For I am a man of unclean lips" (6:5). The depth and passion of Isaiah's conviction sounds like reverent shame to me, a recognition of unworthiness before God.

To Isaiah's reference to lips, we could add Moses taking off his sandals and Joshua "[tearing] his clothes and [falling] facedown to the ground before the ark of the LORD" (Joshua 7:6). There's something physical in true reverence, something that involves our whole person, not just a mind saying certain things to itself or to God. More than other aspects of reverence, shame seems to move us bodily. We respond with our whole being—shaking, falling on our knees or crying—because we know who we are in contrast to a holiness that is so much higher and purer.

In many therapeutic circles, "good shame" is an oxymoron. Most counselors can't bring themselves to bless any form of shame, because their offices are filled with folks who are tormented by it. And there *is* bad shame. Finger-wagging parents shame their children into good works. Some of us feel such self-contempt that we don't believe we have anything to offer in a conversation. For those with eating disorders, candy bars and hamburgers prompt grossly exaggerated shame. When I call shame an appropriate manifesta-

tion of reverence, I am in no way blessing these misplaced accusations—and if you'd rather use the word *guilt* or *conscience* instead
of *shame*, that's fine with me.

But I believe there is reverent shame. If living every day in deep
regret is destructive, might it also be harmful to *never* feel regret?
Reverent shame—or guilt—says, "My Lord and God, I don't deserve the grace you offer through Jesus. The gift of your love makes
me want to live as well as I can."

Shamelessness turns us into moral lepers. We lose our moral
warning system. Because leprosy kills the nerves that tell lepers
they are putting their hands on something hot or sharp, lepers get
hurt. Without the good shame a strong conscience provides, we
get hurt too. We become so accepting, so tolerant, that instead of
stopping at envy, we go ahead and steal; instead of stopping at lust,
we go ahead and flirt, meet for coffee and have an affair. Good
shame reminds us to ask God for help so that we don't wander
from him.

Standing up to the profane sometimes begins with shame. Our
conscience might lead us to resist deplorable advertising or a slan-
derous joke or a wrongheaded claim in a film. We might also feel
ashamed of Christians who give Jesus a bad name. Some are self-
righteous and too easily miffed—in part because their whole way
of being seems to be "against"—against the political left or right,
against cults or atheists, against evolution or the environmentally
insensitive. Against, against, against. They criticize fanatical Mus-
lim fundamentalists then lead jihads themselves. For shame.

Reverence as awe. Recently, when a waitress asked me what I
would like to drink and I said, "Lemonade," she responded with,
"Awesome!" Even in our hyperbole-happy culture, this word
struck me as ridiculously misplaced. Reverent awe, I think, is a
sense of inspired wonder, of amazement at what is beyond us
(God), or a blissful recognition of what is right in front of us (God's
actions). After Jesus healed a paralyzed man, Luke reports in his

Gospel, "Everyone was amazed and gave praise to God. They were filled with awe and said, 'We have seen remarkable things today'" (5:26). To be in awe is to feel the large goodness of God; it's to get caught up in the gravity of a sacred moment. As Ben Patterson writes, "Awe and reverence are what you feel when you know the enormity of the stakes involved. . . . When you gather to worship, remind others that God is the lover of our souls, a tender Father, but also a consuming fire—not a God to trifle with." Lemonade is not awesome.

In addition to feeling awe at God's works, we also praise him for his character: "Who among the gods is like you, LORD? Who is like you—majestic in holiness, awesome in glory, working wonders?" (Exodus 15:11). One problem we have with praise-oriented Scriptures is that, as the saying goes, "Familiarity breeds contempt." We are so used to hearing God honored that it sounds like so much "blah, blah, blah" to us. Here's one test: did you study the two Scriptures just mentioned, or did you skim them, thinking, "I already know all this"?

If you skimmed these texts (as I often do), read this next one carefully: "'Your wickedness will punish you; your backsliding will rebuke you. Consider then and realize how evil and bitter it is for you when you forsake the LORD your God and have no awe of me,' declares the Lord, the LORD Almighty" (Jeremiah 2:19). I'm not equating our breezy reading with wickedness that deserves punishment; I want to highlight the expectation that God has to be regarded with awe. We *should* be in awe. If we aren't, the problem is not with God.

Part of what diminishes awe is mindless repetition—and technology has greatly increased our ability to repeat what we enjoy. We can pause live TV. We can even replay a song we love until we are sick of it. In the novel *Perelandra*, the main character, Ransom, travels to Venus and tastes a fruit so delicious he realizes that, back on Earth, wars would be fought for it. Though his hunger had

been fully satisfied by it, he reaches for another one and nearly
plucks it. Then he sees that such a "repetition would be a vulgarity—
like asking to hear the same symphony twice in a day." Though
liturgy can be evocative, thoughtless repetition can desensitize
us. Kneeling can become rote. Genuine awe resists meaningless
routine.

Reverence as respect. When I was a boy, I was told to wipe my
feet at the door on the way into the house. Today our kids and
their friends take off their shoes and leave them in a pile at the
entry. Because a carpet is valuable, its beauty should be respected.
It's not holy ground, but it sure gets defiled easily. Too bad we
don't always treat God as respectfully as we treat carpet.

Respect has something to do with recognizing high status—
and doing our best to honor that person or object. What do we
respect these days? Uncommon courage and sacrifice. Wealth and
power, to be sure. But in many ways, respect has fallen on hard
times. Casual Friday has become Casual Week, Casual Year and
Casual Life. For all the good change toward approachability and
comfort, we struggle to give proper deference to the sacred. We are
nice to God. We offer thanks before meals and go to worship once
a week. But, I ask myself, do I treat God *better* than I treat the
person on the planet I most respect?

In Malachi 1:8, God shows what this might mean. About bring-
ing sacrifices to the altar, he says, "When you offer blind animals
for sacrifice, is that not wrong? When you sacrifice lame or dis-
eased animals, is that not wrong? Try offering them to your gover-
nor! Would he be pleased with you? Would he accept you?' says
the LORD Almighty." Giving our best to the Creator of the universe
makes good sense.

Yet reverent respect is not absolute. We need not feel compelled
to respect incompetent leaders or discriminatory laws, as if injustice should be treated well. Sometimes respect for God will look
like disrespect to others. It's called standing up to the profane,

speaking in a loving but clear prophetic voice. Reverent respect means rejecting false claims to authority. It means gently, firmly and redemptively standing up to those who are given too much power in our culture.

History is filled with examples. Whereas Luther said "here I stand" against the profane abuses of the papacy, Ignatius stood against sacrilege from within the Roman Catholic Church. Theodore Weld and William Wilberforce resisted the profane act of slavery. Dorothy Day and Mother Teresa worked against the profanity of poverty. Many today see environmental stewardship as a way of being reverent.

One deity in our time that deserves opposition is the god of youth. Worshipers accept as true that each year over the age of twenty-four creates more distance from holy perfection. Believers in this cult follow the Doctrine of Adolescent Standards. What the young deem important is important; what they choose to buy is worthy of expenditure; the body should, no matter what age, conform to the physical features of these years; and all that really matters is "being in love." Perceptively, my daughter Emily asked in sixth grade, "Why are all the songs on the radio about romance? Isn't there anything else to sing about?"

Resisting the cult of youth would include highlighting and protesting the marginalization of the elderly, the denigration of parental authority and the pervasive sense of entitlement in the young. We need to encourage women to stop genuflecting before the altars of holy thinness, the makeup counter and the fashion sections of magazines. It's time to tell men in their twenties to stop worshiping boyish irresponsibility and to cease their devotion to self-centered leisure. Like the old Chinese practice of foot binding, these choices can harm the body. They can also delay emotional and spiritual maturation.

Reverence as gratitude. Years ago, my wife and I were shopping for a large car for our family of five. Although we wanted a gas-

saving, status-enhancing, newer foreign car, we searched for a
wide-bodied cruiser. We discovered that a man in our church
wanted to replace his two-shades-of-beige Chevy. So we discussed
a price and waited for him to settle the transaction. But week upon
week, we didn't hear back from him. Since we needed the car for
an imminent cross-country trip, I decided to ask again: "I don't
mean to put any pressure on you to sell your car to us, but because
of our trip, we need to know if we can buy your car or if we should
keep looking."

He said, "Oh, we have no intention of selling you our car."

My heart sank.

He took a breath and said, "My wife and I are going to give it to
you."

During the years we drove that car, every mile felt like an un-
merited gift—and we were transformed by the experience. Gratitude is part of reverence because something in us needs to acknowledge God's generosity. Mercifully, "he remembers that we
are dust" (Psalm 103:14), and he sent his Son as a sacrifice for us.
How can we not revere this Lord with gratitude?

What would you do if you slipped on a roof and rolled down,
screaming toward the edge, only to fall into someone's arms? Well,
I knew what to do. I looked up at my dad and said, "Thanks!"
Then I called my relatives and my friends. I told anyone who
would listen. Gratitude seeks expression. Many psalmists say
something like, "Sing to the LORD with grateful praise" (147:7).
Jonah 2:9 says, "But I, with shouts of grateful praise, will sacrifice
to you. . . . 'Salvation comes from the LORD.'" And in Colossians we
read that worship includes singing with "gratitude in your hearts"
(3:16). If I overflow with praise when saved from a roof, how much
more so when I know I've been forgiven?

I'm happy to report that gratefulness can be learned. For years,
my friend Lori Coleman has led what she calls Grateful Hearts
groups. In them, she fosters an appreciation for all of God's gifts,

encouraging others to notice the sacred around them, even while working at an unsatisfying job or gardening at home. She means to cultivate a reverence-based gratitude that accentuates everyday goodness. Regarding her father who died when she was young, Lori says that she has a choice to complain about the years she did not have with him or to be grateful for the years she did have. This kind of choice presents itself many times a day. As Thomas Merton said, "The full fruitfulness of spiritual life begins in gratitude for life, in the consent to live, and in the greater gratitude that seeks to be dissolved and to be with Christ."

Reverence as joy. In *Telling the Truth*, Frederick Buechner discusses the gospel as tragedy, comedy and fairy tale. The tragic truth is plain enough: We all have "evil in the imagination" of our hearts, and we are all "at least eight parts chicken, phony, slob." The gospel as fairy tale is Buechner's way of talking about eternal life, the "happily ever after" of God's design for our lives. But the "gospel as comedy" can cause some confusion. The comedy is that, despite our wrongdoing, we are "loved anyway, cherished, forgiven, bleeding to be sure, but also bled for." Buechner says that this fact can be seen as a kind of splendid joke, a comedy that should lead to smiles and outright laughter.

When I teach from Buechner's book, my students and I often stumble over the idea of the gospel as holy humor. We feel unsettled, disturbed. Since many punch lines have an element of ridicule, Buechner's proposal seems, dare I say it, irreverent. However, after twenty years of thinking about this concept, I think I am beginning to get it—and "getting the joke" is an important step along the continuum of reverence.

The gospel *is* funny, in a that's-so-ridiculous-I-can't-help-but-laugh sort of way. Buechner imagines Abraham and Sarah receiving the news that she would conceive and bear a child—at age ninety. In that pre-Viagra era, their laughter must have filled the tent. The whole idea of it is sincerely laughable—and seriously

reverent. In fact, I'm ready to say that *not* to see the humor in it
may be irreverent.

Our view is often too somber. We hear "reverence" and think of
monks chanting around the cloister or Puritans sternly proclaiming a holy God. Why should we think otherwise? No one smiles in
a "holy" painting. But a fuller view would also imagine monks
smiling over a novice's silly mistake and Puritans offering a toast at
a harvest party. Sometimes, when I am grieving or depressed, I feel
the beginnings of joy springing up. In my darkness, one impulse I
have is to suppress the joy, reasoning that things are just too bleak
for it. Joy seems inappropriate, as if it doesn't grasp the magnitude
of the pain. But if present circumstances are too dreary to permit
joy, then joy has never been permissible, for surely every age before
us has suffered as much or more than ours. I don't begrudge others
their joy; neither should I oppose it in myself. Years ago, I heard
that the great Ugandan bishop Festo Kivengere said that one of the
marks of followers of Jesus is that they laugh easily.

Reverence finds its end in joy. That's where it most feels at
home. Fear may be the beginning, but "perfect love drives out
fear" (1 John 4:18). In this life, we never lose all cause for good
fear, but as our knowledge of and relationship with God mature,
we will know the love of God and find ourselves expressing joy
more and more often. How preposterous is this: The Son of God
becomes an infant who giggles and needs his diapers changed.
The Creator of fir, cedar and oak is the Father of an ordinary car-
penter from a poor, obscure village, a man who dies on a wooden
cross. This same God makes us the beneficiaries of his trust fund.
We, the morally impoverished, are in line for an inheritance so
rich, billionaires would be embarrassed. We've won the spiritual
lottery! Ha, it's all a joke, right? Yes, but a true one.

How can we possibly do justice to all of this outlandishness?
With a joyful reverence. Psalm 5:11 says, "Let all who take refuge
in [the Lord] be glad; let them ever sing for joy." And Psalm 126:3

says, "The LORD has done great things for us, and we are filled with joy." Should all this good news fill us with sorrow, dreariness and horror? Why not a beaming grin?

Luke reports in his Gospel that Jesus felt this kind of reverence: "Jesus, *full of joy* through the Holy Spirit, said, 'I praise you, Father, Lord of heaven and earth, because you have hidden these things from the wise and learned, and revealed them to little children. Yes, Father, for this was *your good pleasure*'" (10:21, italics mine). To be sure, Jesus was a Man of Sorrows, but he also was—and is—a Man of Mirth. He knows he can heal the brokenhearted, and one day he will return to set things right again. So, we smile and feel joy—and joy is usually expressed in praise. Joy expresses reverence because when we see that a holy God loves us, we know how laugh-out-loud merciful he is.

MOVING ALONG THE CONTINUUM

When reverence says that the sacred deserves responses from fear to joy, it tells a particular truth about God in each case. If our Lord is a God to be feared (at least some of the time), what does this response tell us about God? He is fearsome. He is powerful, able to cherish or to banish. Shame tells us that God is good, that he is moral, that he cares about our choices. In a state of awe, we learn that God is inspiring, majestic and beautiful. When we respect God, we are saying he is worthy of allegiance, of obedience, that his leadership is supreme. Gratitude recognizes God's goodness, his sacrificial giving. It acknowledges that God gives us what we haven't earned. Joy tells us that God is love, that he is the source of all good pleasure and that he enriches our lives beyond measure.

And we move from left to right. That's why the phrase comes in Scripture—at least twenty-seven times—"Do not be afraid." One of these is the angel announcing Jesus' birth: "I bring you good news of great joy that will be for all the people" (Luke 2:10). Fear and shame will be left behind in heaven. Psalm 34 captures this sentiment: "I sought the LORD, and he answered me; he delivered me from all my fears. Those who look to him are radiant; their faces are never covered with shame" (vv. 4-5). And the writer of Hebrews says, "Since we are receiving a kingdom that cannot be shaken, let us be thankful, and so worship God acceptably with reverence and awe" (12:28).

In the section on fear, I told the story of a professor who said he was being kind by telling me my answer was "interesting." My dread of Dr. LaRusso made me want to avoid him altogether, but I had to take classes from him. In these, I felt ashamed of the quality of my work, and I often turned it in sheepishly. At the same time, I was in awe of his teaching. He lectured majestically, asked questions perceptively and taught with more wisdom than I usually heard from the pulpit.

Because of my respect for him, I sought his counsel, but I waited for it, sometimes sitting outside his office for hours until he was free. When I would finally take a seat facing him, he gave me his complete attention—and I was immensely grateful for his presence and what he said to me. Our relationship matured. By the time I received my degree, I called him by his first name, Dominic, and we laughed often. What began with fear had moved through shame and awe, and into respect, gratefulness and joy.

And so it is with the Teacher of teachers, the Lord Jesus. Our reverence manifests itself in various ways, as our life with him calls various responses out of us. When Dominic died, I lost one of the most influential people in my life. I count it a privilege today to teach "in his name." When Jesus died, we didn't lose him. We gained redemption and the presence of his Spirit. Our privilege is to live each minute "in his name."

❧ THE DISCIPLINE OF ASTONISHMENT

I admit it. I love G. K. Chesterton. I can't say for certain we'll be on a first-name basis, but I hope to have many a chat with him in some heavenly pub. I visited one of his earthly "haunts" in London, Ye Olde Cheshire Cheese, just off Fleet Street. Sitting in a booth, I imagined his playful, three-hundred-pound presence across from me, spouting wisdom and making me laugh. Many of his ideas have burrowed deep into my soul, and I would be remiss not to give him considerable credit for inspiring my idea here that the discipline that aids the practice of reverence is *astonishment*.

Chesterton wrote about the joy he felt in "the sacred intoxication of existence." Maybe he spent just a little too much time in that pub, but I think he is right. We should be nearly drunk with delight over what we are permitted to experience. In this spirit, I offer the discipline of astonishment as *the willful appreciation for the miracle of the ordinary*. We might also call it a quick-to-be-amazed responsiveness. Chesterton sees God's world as a place worthy of admiration, from the roundness of river stones to the glories of a toasted muffin. He says, "How can we contrive to be at once astonished at the world and yet at home in it? . . . I wish to set forth my faith as particularly answering this double spiritual need, the need for that mixture of the familiar and the unfamiliar which Christendom has rightly named romance."

Too often we lose this inquisitiveness and appreciation. It gets chastised out of us by cynics and rulemongers, and sometimes even by our teachers or parents. We grow dull to the miracle in the ordinary, and we take things for granted. When we lose astonishment, our reverence suffers.

Few acts elicit spontaneous gratitude more assuredly than a surprising grace. And this is just the point: Our lives are filled with surprising grace. All day long, we are receiving. The question is, Do we feel astonishment? Do we appreciate the ordinary as a daily miracle? Being surprised has everything to do with our expectations. If we know we don't deserve gift upon gift, we will stand amazed at the bounty we receive—and will honor the Sender. Astonishment doesn't just happen to us; it can be chosen.

My main model for this discipline is my daughter Laura, who always has approached life as if everything in her path was created for her enjoyment. As a child, she would be thrilled by most anything: an empty photo album that could be filled with her stories or salt and pepper shakers that she turned into people talking and knocking heads. Now in her twenties, Laura still sees simple pleasures as sacred. She does not feel entitled. She feels blessed by the daily miracles of life. How can we all learn better astonishment?

Cultivating the illusion of the first time. In the first pages of *Orthodoxy*, Chesterton imagines an explorer setting off from England to discover a new island in the South Seas. His boat gets blown off course and lands him right back where he started, at Brighton Beach, but the explorer thinks he is on uncharted territory. How differently he sees that place, as if for the first time.

Without actually sailing away, we can cultivate an illusion of the first time, remembering our initial thrill at new experiences and coming at the familiar in unfamiliar ways. It's a way of stimulating astonishment at what we previously took for granted. We can create this illusion by changing something routine, by traveling a different route to work or by emphasizing smell instead of sight during a walk. We can also concentrate our imagination, picturing ourselves as if we are just now seeing for the first time a place that's grown old to us. Inevitably, we see something we've missed, and this discovery can lead to a reverent awe or gratitude.

How sad that our reverence becomes rote and dreary, that we are not flabbergasted by the goodness of the Father or stunned by the sacrifice of Jesus or overwhelmed that the Spirit "himself intercedes for us through wordless groans" (Romans 8:26). But we don't have to stay in a flabbergast-deprived state. We might be more astonished if we cultivated the illusion of the first time during worship. If you sit in the same place every Sunday, vary your landing spot. If you tend to be chatty before the service, try being silent. If your devotional life is 99 percent reading and 1 percent prayer, reverse the ratio. And on and on. Of course, the most important choice is to give ourselves fully to what is happening. Don't sit passively waiting for leaders to be so amazing that they move you. Sing as if it's your first song to Jesus. Hear the Word as if it had just been translated into your language. It's a choice. We can choose to be astonished, and reverence will likely follow.

Cultivating the illusion of the last time. Like "the first time," isn't "the last time" usually an intense experience? As an undergrad, I loved the three hundred acres I lived on for three years, affectionately known as The Ranch. The adobe house had walls over two feet thick, a gravity-fed water supply and a cut-out fifty-five-gallon drum for the only source of heat. What wasn't to love? On my last day there, I walked the property, taking everything in and cherishing it. I held tightly to the call of the killdeer sweeping low over the grassy hills, the throbbing pulse of the train passing nearby and the sight of the funny pictures we'd varnished into the wood floor in the kitchen. I stood amazed at what God had permitted me to enjoy.

But we don't have to leave to imagine leaving. We can cultivate the *illusion* of the last time—and in so doing foster reverence. As a young father, when I traveled without my family, I often found myself sitting in an airport ruminating on what life would be like if something terrible were to happen to my wife and kids while I was away. Morbid, I know, but it had good effect. When I greeted my family again, I swept them gratefully into my arms. We increase our appreciation for the ordinary when we imagine it being lost.

Astonished by the sacred. Of course, God's character and goodness are astonishing, but we can see his sanctity elsewhere as well. The great rabbi Abraham Heschel wrote that we are called "to be a witness to the holy, to give testimony to the grandeur of honesty, to the glory of righteousness, to the holiness of truth, to the marvel and mystery of being alive." Some Protestants bristle at the thought of respecting anything as holy except God, but many things are called holy in the New Testament. There are references to the holy place, holy city, holy angels, holy prophets, holy ground, holy Scriptures, holy law, holy temple, holy calling and even a holy kiss. (But note, there is no holy cow.)

With eyes to see the sacred, we see it. In *Refuge*, Terry Tempest Williams writes, "It's strange how deserts turn us into believers. I believe in walking in a landscape of mirages, because you learn humility. . . . If the desert is holy, it is because it is a forgotten place that allows us to remember the sacred." And when we express reverence for a particular place, we respect it and what it means to those who live there.

For years, I've been intrigued by St. Augustine's statement that "only God can be loved for his own sake." He means that our love is easily misplaced, that when we love others for their sake, we tend to get possessive or not act in their best interests, and when we love nature for its sake, we can deify it and lose sight of God. This perspective keeps astonishment moving us to kneel before God and not something less.

Astonished by the profane. A music CD cover pictures the recording artist in a crown of thorns. A magazine cover announces "The Good Girl's Guide to Bad-Girl Sex." A mining company strips a beautiful hillside down to rubble. Are we astonished? Usually not, but if we were, might we more often stand up to the profane, at least to mention something in conversation?

If only we weren't so desensitized. If only a trampling of God felt like someone walking over us. When Mother Teresa was asked how she could lift the dying from Calcutta's gutters, she said she saw "Christ in distressing disguise." When she looked at the poorest of the poor, she saw the profanation of Jesus neglected and mistreated. We can all hope that our neighbors don't need to be dying for us to practice this reverent perspective.

Lesser known is Graham Greene's lens-shifting phrase in *The Power and the Glory*. As an old priest struggles to love a smelly, unattractive vagabond, he decides to replace every reference to the wanderer with "God's image," as in, "God's image shook now" and "upon the shoulders of God's image." In such a renaming, we might be astonished at God's image instead of dulled to it. What if I said,

> On the sidewalk in my town, the image of God begs for
>   money.
> In my classroom, an image of God asks me a question.
> Right now, an image of God is reading my book.

Astonishing!

How else might astonishment help us see the profane? Hiking near Death Valley years ago, my friend and I scrambled over a shale-slippery slope to get to a rare waterfall. Awed by God's creativity, we sat on a small patch of wild, green grass and took in this wonder of the world—until we saw the trash. Beer cans, junkfood wrappers and broken glass littered the place, the inevitable detritus of human presence. There was one good word for it: irreverence. At least that will be a good word for it as long as we are astonished by the trash. When we accept the profane, when we say "that's just the way things are these days," we will eventually stop calling anything profane and stop standing up to it. There will be nothing we deem worth resisting. It's called decadence.

But astonishment can be cultivated. More than we realize, it is an act of the will. Typically, Christians "give thanks" for their food and sometimes for "the hands that prepared it." Some native peoples also give thanks to the animal that "gave up" its life so that they might eat. This gratefulness might seem far-fetched to those of us who live our days in technological dependence, but the act points toward a habit of reverence, a choice to acknowledge the sacred in God's astonishing work. Cultivating illusions of the first and last times will help.

Let us together learn to respond to God with reverence. Let us, in faith, kneel before the sacred and stand up to the profane, accentuating our astonishment of God's person, words and works. Let us learn to say with David, "Praise the LORD, O my soul; all my inmost being, praise his holy name" (Psalm 103:1).

FOR DISCUSSION OR REFLECTION

1. In our culture, where do you see reverence or irreverence? What are our objects of worship and objects of ridicule? What is your stance toward or involvement with these trends?

2. What is the condition of your kneeling before the sacred? How do you express deference to God's holiness?

3. What in our world would you call profane? What would it mean to stand up to these profanations? Discuss your lists with others, and—just as importantly—discuss constructive ways we can have these conversations.

4. Discuss the virtue of reverence in your life along the points of the continuum. Are you moving from left to right? Also,

   a. When might contemporary followers of Jesus need to express a healthy fear?

   b. What is the role of good shame in your life? Explain your relationship to the concept of "moral leprosy."

   c. About what do you feel awe? Do you relate your appreciation to God? Is your sense of what is awesome too loose, too inclusive?

    d. How does respect's "bringing our best to God" relate to your life?

    e. Discuss a situation in which you consciously chose gratefulness. Contrast it with a situation marked by bitterness. How do these choices relate to reverence?

    f. How do you relate to the idea of the gospel as a glorious joke? If you resist this idea, in what sense might your resistance reveal a stuffy view of God?

5. Jesus' actions struck a number of his contemporaries as irreverent. Can you reconcile his irreverence with his reverence? Explain.

EXERCISE

1. Read a passage of Scripture aloud, as if for the first time. Try reading it in different ways: sadly, gleefully, sternly, passionately. Then read it as if tomorrow your Bible will be taken away forever. Record your thoughts.

2. Pray in different physical postures that seem to connect to the six points on the continuum from fear to joy. You might prostrate yourself in fear, bow in shame, kneel in awe and so on.

7 ❧ CONTENTMENT

don't care how; I want it now!

Who is rich? He that is content.

Who is that? Nobody.

BENJAMIN FRANKLIN

I am a privileged person. I am a well-educated, white, middle-class, happily married man with three terrific daughters. Let's face it, I'm not exactly from a marginalized group. Living in a beautiful city with its temperate climate, I can walk to my usually rewarding job. I have more "blessings" than most people who have occupied the planet for the last ten thousand years.

Yet I complain.

Sometimes my coffee gets cold and I have to reheat it. Several times. When stress is building and I'm late for an important event, I get frustrated and angry. And I worry that I haven't been a good enough husband or father, that I haven't sufficiently served the needy, that my novels haven't sold well enough, that my wife and I won't have enough money for retirement, that my knees won't let me keep playing tennis—or that this book will have too many long and burdensome sentences.

In more reasoned moments, I think, "What will it take for me to be content? Don't I have enough?" Ben Franklin's words ring true. No one is content, at least very few of us.

Of course, we have good cause to be anxious about the economy and our income, global disaster and the future of the planet. And some have suffered beyond our darkest fears: the enslaved, the raped, the homeless—or my colleague whose wife died from brain cancer three years after their son committed suicide. When I hear of these struggles, I pray, and I shake my fist.

Most of us worry. A lot. It's hard to be content in our times, maybe harder than at any other time in human history. Sometimes I feel like I'm battling a thousand charging soldiers, and all I've got is a cardboard shield and a paper sword.

QUESTIONS ABOUT THE GOOD LIFE

Before we get to the major aspects of contentment, I want to inquire about a few issues related to desire:

- When you hear the word *desire* do you think of something sexual or romantic in nature? Or do you think of wanting to change the world for the better?

- When you consider the Good Life, do you imagine a large house, a fine car, a spouse so fantastic that your friends faint— or do you think of the place where you are sitting right now?

- Let's suppose that your favorite neighborhood wish-granting fairy comes to you and says, "I'll give you one of two choices. You can have a perfect body, the face and figure and muscle tone you've always wanted—and you will *never* need to exercise or diet to maintain this body—or you can have perfect humility. So, what will it be: the perfect body or perfect humility?"

Of course, you know the right answer to that last one. You don't want to look shallow, and you know that if you had perfect humility you wouldn't worry about your looks. But the real question— the question behind the question—is, Which occupies more of your time: desiring a perfect body or desiring perfect humility? Have you ever *longed* for greater humility?

Okay, enough guilt. My point is not to have us wallow in the misery of our choices. It is to get us thinking about various terms related to contentment, such as desire, longing, covetousness, ambition, passion and lust. Desire, like most things, can be a blessing or a curse. Without it, we would never get out of bed in the morning. With it, we've achieved the loveliest good and the most despicable evil. Longing isn't wrong, but we can long wrongly.

DESIRE: AS SEEN ON TV!

Though our desires are best when directed by love, advertising culture seems to be committed to our discontentment, determined to sucker us into the lowest versions of desire. Not only is "Desire" a perfume that can be purchased, it has become an urge that can and should be satisfied with products. Want to impress others? Get this jacket. Yearn for a good family? Buy a new car. Hope to stimulate the opposite sex? Purchase this ring or go see this movie or eat this food or use this wrench or, come to think of it, buy just about anything. If this orientation is inevitable in a capitalist economy, a good question to keep before us is, "What is being sold to me?"

Too often we talk as if products will solve all our problems. We say,

- Shop till you drop.
- You have to sell yourself if you want to get ahead.
- That's money in the bank.
- That's rich.
- It's just business.
- Do you think I'm made of money?
- I'm investing in people.

We can even say, "You have *sold out* to consumerism," or "you have *bought into* the materialistic worldview." That is, if you like irony.

If asked "Does money buy happiness?" we say no. Then we add, "But it doesn't hurt." It's the American Dream, isn't it? When travelers say, "I can't believe how little money Ugandans have, and how content they are," we nod our heads knowingly and say, "Yeah, we have a lot to learn from them." Although we believe they could teach us, we wouldn't trade our more materially prosperous lives for all the familial love and contentment in Uganda—or China or anywhere else. At the same time, some of us aren't feeling prosperous at all these days. Some have even declared bankruptcy. Whether in relative riches or want, what is the source of our hope?

The almighty if. I don't know about you, but if I just had X, I would be happy. If I had another $100,000 or if my favorite team would win a championship. And so it goes for most of us. If we could just get a new kitchen floor or whiter teeth or better-behaved kids or more education. Of course, the problem is that when we get what we want, when the *if* is satisfied, the satisfaction lasts no longer than the aftertaste from the last drop of our favorite drink. We want another sip, a longer gulp, a constant drip of tastiness.

Sometimes I think that all our struggles with contentment come down to this one word: *if*. What makes confronting this word difficult is that most of the time we don't care in the slightest about being content. We want to be happy, but in our minds that means desiring things and acquiring them. Yet is all this crying after stuff actually a cry of desperation, a cry for help? Maybe we do want contentment but we are afraid of how we might need to change.

Volunteers not victims. We cope by ridiculing the emptiness and banality of the way things are sold to us, but, as historian Daniel Boorstin notes, "The deeper problems connected with advertising come less from . . . the desire to seduce than from the desire to be seduced." We work to be in a position to give in to the promises we've been sold. We grumble that we are being drafted, then we go out and enlist. For the most part, we aren't victims of an overpowering consumerist culture, we're volunteers. We've joined up and are happy to be onboard.

Advertising is the largest business in America—with companies collectively spending in the triple-digit billions—yet I have never met a single person who admits to purchasing a product solely because of advertising. I don't admit it either. Perhaps the greatest achievement of advertising is that those who are influenced by it are certain they are not.

DESIRE: I LUST YOU. I LUST YOU VERY MUCH.

Down the hall or down the street lives The Beautiful One. This neighbor is startlingly well put together physically, financially, psychologically. We wish we could be The Beautiful One, with the same qualities and the same stuff. Barring that, we want him or her for ourselves, to love us with abandon, the sooner the better.

Ah, lust. It makes loving our neighbor so difficult. Frederick Buechner calls lust "the craving for salt of a man who is dying of thirst." Another word for corrupted desire is *covetousness*, a term that may seem outdated but I suspect mainly feels too strong, too judgmental. It wags its finger at us from Exodus 20:17: "You shall not covet your neighbor's house. You shall not covet your neighbor's wife, or his male or female servant, his ox or donkey, or anything that belongs to your neighbor." Depending on where you live and how many donkeys live next door, you might not think this commandment pertains directly to you, but the spirit of the commandment is that God cares about our motivations because, if misplaced, they can ruin just about anything.

The hard messages here are that discontentment is disobedience and that covetousness includes all the twisted ways we wish we had what belongs to someone else. Most of the time, we aren't as flagrant a commandment breaker as Veruca Salt in the movie

Willy Wonka and the Chocolate Factory, who sings, "Don't care how; I want it now!" But no matter how much subtler we become, coveting can corrupt. As we daydream about physically hurting an enemy, getting a sexy body into bed or eating ourselves into oblivion, we grow closer to violence, adultery or gluttony. Coveting what can't be ours—his garden, her cheekbones, their "normal" children—is ultimately frustrating because some "possessions" are simply out of reach no matter how much talent or money we have.

Much of the time, we feel in need. We never have enough, and we never *are* enough. And we can't blame advertising for these sentiments. Coveting comes from the heart.

DESIRE: THE FASCIST WITHIN

In the classic 1940 film *The Great Dictator,* Charlie Chaplin spoofs Hitler and other fascists in power at the time. Our era has its own ruthless rulers, none of whom would want to hear Chaplin's lead character: "Greed has poisoned men's souls, has barricaded the world with hate, has goose-stepped us into misery and bloodshed. . . . Dictators free themselves, but they enslave the people!" We may not have suffered under a political fascist, but I think that all of us must contend with our own totalitarian impulse. Inside our souls is a little dictator who wants to rule the little situations in the little communities of our little world. No, I am not claiming that you are the next Hitler, just that if you gave full freedom to your desire for control and if you had opportunity and charisma and military backing, you might demand that things go exactly as you want them to. Being in control. Don't you love it?

Micromanaging our circumstances is one of the primary obstacles to contentment. Much of our world defies control. Roommates. Careers. Health. Getting kids to do their homework. Doing our own homework. Most of the time, we can't *make* things go our way—and the more we deceive ourselves with this "fascist fantasy" of control, the more discontent we will be. The steel beams of circumstance simply won't easily bend to our desires.

Scholar Kenneth Burke says that all humans are "rotten with perfection." He means that it's human nature to seek to fulfill our goals as best as we can. We always want an accurate basketball shot, the best friendship, the "right" word. So, our desire to do the best and manage our lives is not wrong; it is inevitable.

Yet there is a difference between pursuing excellence and expecting things always to be excellent. It's one thing to want to choose the right word; it's another to feel anxious for days over whether or not we did. It's one thing to regret that our first pimple in ten years has to show up right before our big speech; it's another to obsess over every cottage-cheese mark of cellulite. But it's not as if being "out of control" is an admirable goal. The issue is how we control our desire for absolute control.

The Ten Commandments offer help once more. The second one says, "You shall not make for yourself an image in the form of anything in heaven above or on the earth beneath or in the waters below. You shall not bow down to them or worship them; for I, the LORD your God, am a jealous God" (Exodus 20:4-5). The attraction of an idol is that the worshiper gets to be in charge. With the proper incantation, a god possesses the statue and then the worshiper can order the god around. In response to this practice, God says, essentially, "You cannot control me. I am in charge, not you." Most of us would do well to remind ourselves of this truth every day.

But often the power to control—in worship and in other aspects of life—is exactly what we crave. We don't bow to golden calves anymore; we bow to glowing "stars," graven images of celebrities and physical perfection. We idolize romance, respect and idyllic vacations on tropical islands. We fantasize about these things, making ourselves "win" in each situation. Sometimes this means worshiping at their respective altars.

Fantasizing can be terrific. It can allow us to visualize achievement in a way that helps us step in that direction. While nothing is wrong with daydreaming about hitting a home run or scoring an A on a paper or walking happily along a lakeshore with our grandkids, some fantasies grab our totalitarian impulse and puff it up until it inhibits our love for our neighbors. The power fantasy. The romance fantasy. Since the key to fantasy is personal control, we enjoy fantasizing, because in our imagination we get what we want. Unlike real human beings, fantasy bosses and sex partners do not resist our ambitions.

Some say this is fantasy's gift to us. Because fantasies are not populated by real people, we can't hurt anyone in them. We can "have our fun," and the images just go away. But if I let my fantasies become unrestrained, I can end up thinking that my job *should* be fulfilling every minute, that my house *should* look like the ones in the magazines, that my spouse *should* be tantalizing and compliant at all times and never have bad breath. We grow in our belief that we ought to be able to control the world such that it conforms absolutely to our desires—and that's bad for contentment.

DISCONTENTED WHINING

Undisciplined desire: a consumerist vision of the Good Life, a free-flowing covetousness and a totalitarian impulse that fosters idolatry. The result? Discontentment in the form of whining and worry. This bed is too soft. The pastor is boring. My boss is an idiot. If you are thinking, *Oh yes, I know a few obnoxious whiners,* consider this amazing discovery: researchers Robert Kegan and Lisa Lahey report that "complaint" is the most common way employees talk to each other, even when job morale is high. Imagine what whining is like in an office with low job satisfaction!

Puritan Jeremiah Burroughs challenges us: "To be discontented in any afflicted condition is sinful and evil, but to be discontented when we are in the midst of God's mercies, when we are not able to count the mercies of God, still to be discontented because we have not got all we would have, this is a greater evil." Is this view of "murmuring," as Burroughs calls it, too inclusive? Is every complaint of mine disobedience? Isn't there a difference between complaining about an injustice and complaining about the traffic?

Perhaps Paul clarifies these issues by saying that "the love of money is a root of all kinds of evil" (1 Timothy 6:10). It's the greed, the envy, the ungratefulness for what we have been given, not the money itself. Differences between discontent and healthy criticism have to do with tone, goal and motive. Whining about a pesky gnat is not the same as protesting human trafficking. When we can't tell the difference, when all pebbles in our path seem like Great Boulders of Injustice, we have an overstated sense of deservedness.

Adolescents are famous for feeling entitled, for believing that money and car keys should always be at their disposal. In fact, a local teenager's nickname for his dad was "The Wallet." My experience is that when I am not asking, "Why has God given so much to me?" I am asking impatiently, "Why don't I have more?" My arguments really haven't changed much from my teenage years. I still think I deserve a break—or five. Don't you?

DISCONTENTED WORRY

When my daughters said they would be home at midnight, my worry kicked in by 12:15. I wasn't just unhappy they were late. I was worried they got into a car accident or were abducted by an ax-wielding rapist. Fathers are gifted in anxiety-inflating irrationality. In the Sermon on the Mount, Jesus addresses this kind of discontentment:

> Therefore I tell you, do not worry about your life, what you
> will eat or drink; or about your body, what you will wear.
> . . . Can any one of you by worrying add a single hour to your
> life . . . you of little faith? So do not worry, saying, "What

shall we eat . . . drink . . . wear?" . . . Your heavenly Father
knows that you need them. But seek first his kingdom and
his righteousness, and all these things will be given to you as
well. Therefore do not worry about tomorrow, for tomorrow
will worry about itself. Each day has enough trouble of its
own. (Matthew 6:25, 27, 30-34)

I have a hard time believing that Jesus expects us never to
worry or that all worry is a sin. The world unloads on us too much
hardship. But I do believe he wants us to see good reasons not to
worry. Therefore, Jesus presents us with a choice. We can either
worry or we can seek the kingdom of God. We can fret and stew
and imagine every terrible thing that might occur. Broken bones.
Avalanches. Children slipping off the edge of the Grand Canyon.
Or we can use the same nervous energy to pursue God and his
ways of living, and spend time with others in our community attempting to do the same. We can't just "not worry." Whatever
event consumes us with worry, we have to replace it with heartfelt, well-reasoned talk and silence and prayer and fellowship.

Here's another way to look at this choice. Life is a road trip. On
the open highway, we kick back and sing along with the music.
But, inevitably, we run into a traffic jam. In this moment, we have
a decision to make. Do we zip back and forth from lane to lane,
tailgating, narrowly missing other cars, honking, yelling and
pretty much making a nuisance of ourselves? Or do we pretty
much stay in our lane and trust that things will smooth out? The
irony is that, typically, when the traffic clears, the two cars are in
roughly the same place. Destination-Crazed Commuters may be a
few hundred yards ahead of the Road-Wise Ramblers, but that distance won't matter in the end. What matters is the condition of the
drivers and of all their fellow travelers. Crazed Commuters usually feel agitated and angry—as do those traveling with them.
Most of the time, worry is a lot of effort that profits little.

Worry as a waste of time. Jesus says that worry usually accomplishes a big fat nothing; it cannot add a single hour to your life (Matthew 6:27). Worry doesn't put you at the head of the line of cars or give you more resources for solving your problems. Occasionally, worry might motivate us to necessary action, but healthier motivators exist: shrewd foresight and faith-filled concern. We hold on to our worry because we feel we've earned the right to worry and, doggone it, we are not going to let it go. But most of the time, worry is like screaming at the slow car in front of us even though the car is not going to make us late. Though worry seems like it "can't be helped" in many circumstances, it rarely improves the situation.

Part of the problem is that worry has no discretion. We think that when we have lifted off a large burden, we will be free. But worry is a demon that does not care what it eats. Toss aside the main dish of finances, and worry will happily gobble away at the salad of marriage or the dessert of potential accidents. The issue isn't the issue itself as much as our way of feeding the issue.

Another part of the problem is that though we worry in the present, our worries are mainly about the future, a period of time that we *never* experience. Jerry Sittser says, "Worry can . . . cause problems . . . [because it] is rooted in unreality. When we worry about the future, we worry about something that does not yet exist." Worry is based on various predictions of what might occur— and the overwhelming evidence is that we are lousy prophets. Ninety-nine percent of the awful things we predict never occur. I worry that the airplane will crash. The rash on my arm is actually skin cancer. I'll never find my house keys, which probably fell to the ground and were picked up by a serial killer who followed me home and is now waiting for me inside the house.

The good news is that Jesus does not expect us to be prophets. He wants to liberate us from a future-orientation that corrupts the present: "Do not worry about tomorrow, for tomorrow will worry about itself. Each day has enough trouble of its own" (Matthew 6:34). It's not that bad things never come true. Some people contract painful diseases. Others lose their jobs. Jesus' point is that if we *must* worry, we don't need to worry about the future. Today's troubles are enough to maintain our attention, and at least these troubles are real. When difficulties come, we'll worry plenty. What is gained by all the worry ahead of time? Nothing. Worry is such an unsatisfying way to drive through life.

Does this mean that we should not plan for the future? Should we be so unconcerned that we squander our resources today and end up on the streets? Is Jesus saying, "Live only for today; never give a thought for tomorrow"? I don't think so. But worrying is not the same as planning, and contentment includes the freedom to work toward some future goal—as we shall see.

Worry as a lack of faith. Jesus names another reason for accepting God's version of reality: our heavenly Father knows what we need. This reminds me of an earthly parallel. When putting one of my daughters to bed one night (Emily was probably about seven at the time), she said, "What is faith?" I asked her if she ever worried about whether or not dinner would be on the table or where she might find a place to sleep. She laughed. "Of course not, Daddy, you and Mommy take care of that." I smiled and wished my own faith were as wholehearted. Emily still inspires my faith, helping me see what God might be doing when I am prone to ask why my mother-in-law suffers with Alzheimer's or what good might come out of relationships that are always in crisis.

Our trouble is that, unlike children, we don't like to loosen our white-knuckled grip on the wheel. So Jesus reminds us that the life of the disciple is a life of faith, of trusting that God is love and will do what love calls for. If God is really there, we should pick up our map and follow him—into any desert or snowstorm or squall. But we aren't quite sure God will be with us. Our lack of contentment reveals us to be, as Jesus says, "of little faith" (Matthew 6:30), no matter how justified we feel about our worries. Believing in God's goodness ought to affect the way we face uncertainty.

Jesus' ideas are simple enough. It's the acting upon them that's difficult. And questions about "quality" arise: How do we trust God and push for excellence? Can we be ambitious for something without being defeated by it? Is it possible to possess admirable standards *and* peace of mind? And how can we move toward godliness without becoming self-satisfied or guilt-ridden?

These tensions are significant—and, when added to the other problems I've reviewed, might leave you feeling hunched over under the load. Perhaps my definition of contentment will relieve some of this weight: Contentment is *the strength hope gives us to pursue the unsatisfied life in a satisfying way.* Contentment is a paradox of submissive willfulness; it's an involved detachment.

THE UNSATISFIED LIFE

You might be thinking, *What's so good about the unsatisfied life? That's what I'm trying to avoid!* At face value, I agree, but I mean something a bit below the surface, because the unsatisfied life is not the same as the dissatisfied life.

A difficult world. Living the unsatisfied life means we reckon with the biblical idea that our planet is "fallen," that it is violent and self-seeking, prone to disease and frustration. We know this truth—we've read Genesis 3—but our expectations still scream that things "ought" to go well. In *The Road Less Traveled*, Scott Peck says that many of our disappointments would not exist if we acted as if we believed one phrase: "Life is difficult."

Though Jesus promises an abundant life, he does not say that this life will be easy or get progressively better or entirely fulfill us. We are all going to die. We will all suffer along the way. It's unnerving to think about, so we do what we can to busy ourselves. In his novel *White Noise*, Don DeLillo says, "We're all aware there's no escape from death. How do we deal with this crushing knowledge? We repress, we disguise, we bury, we exclude. Some people do it better than others, that's all." He means that we should stop pretending that we can stay forever young, forever healthy. Although I find joy in my family and job and ministries and hobbies, I experience some measure of "death" every day. What else should I expect? We live in a fallen world. When I live the unsatisfied life well, I tell the truth about the realities of the world's corruptions—and my own.

A troubling world. Civil rights leader Andrew Young tells the story of the Morehouse College days of his friend Martin Luther King Jr. There, college president Benjamin Mays preached once a week, often stating, "God, spare me from the satisfied life." To Mays, the satisfied life was the life of complacency, of resignation. He preached that we should *not* be satisfied with injustice or poverty. He wanted to live the unsatisfied life, the life that did not passively accept discrimination, greed and violence. Living the unsatisfied life means that some things ought to bother us.

A commitment to strong values always leads to an unsettled stance toward unmet standards. To be content, we need not pretend as if everything is just fine. In fact, a complacent contentment is an affront to all who suffer. Some discussions of contentment ignore this. Thomas Carson says that contentment is "being satisfied (or pleased) with one's life." Robert Johnson and Jerry M. Ruhl claim that contentment is "to accept 'what is' instead of insisting that life be a certain way." Acceptance is surely a part of contentment, but what about dissatisfaction with one's own immoral choices or one's government's abuses? George MacDonald captures the paradox well, saying that we should be like God: "easy to please, but hard to satisfy."

Don't we all know people who appear to be content, but are really just trying to be nice and stay out of trouble? Aren't we sometimes these people? Contentment is not the same as being resigned to fate or unmotivated about life or naturally blasé. We can be content and care deeply about the world's problems. Complacency, not contentment, is what keeps us from using our time and money to address poverty, to support the frail and hopeless, and to protect nature as if we believed God made it.

An incomplete world. The writer of Ecclesiastes says,

> I denied myself nothing my eyes desired; I refused my heart no pleasure. My heart took delight in all my labor, and this was the reward for all my toil.
>
> Yet when I surveyed all that my hands had done and what I had toiled to achieve, everything was meaningless, a chasing after the wind; nothing was gained under the sun. (2:10-11)

We've heard this sad story countless times: the small-town kid who makes it big but gambles it all away, the discovered beauty who flames out on drugs, the heiress who squanders opportunities to help others. A commitment to the unsatisfied life means that we reckon with these stories. We truly believe that our happiness will not arrive because we have worked for some glamorous "prize."

The good news about all three aspects of the unsatisfied life is that contentment does not require us to pretend that all is well. Contentment is not blind optimism. We live an unsatisfied life because the world is fallen, because we are troubled by immorality and because we reject empty promises. On one level, we *must* live the unsatisfied life. The question is, How will we live it?

THE PURSUIT

Contentment is the strength hope gives us to pursue the unsatisfied life in a satisfying way. Though unsatisfied, we keep trying. Pursuing, being ambitious for, driving toward, longing after—all these activities are blessed. Paul encourages us to "fight the good fight of the faith" (1 Timothy 6:12). Since life is a struggle, falling short of our goals is no reason to cease striving, any more than we should stop walking because we trip every once in a while. Suggesting we should dispense with our passion would be like saying we should be disembodied.

Interestingly, the "fight the good fight" phrase comes soon after Paul asserts that "godliness with contentment is great gain" (v. 6). In part, Paul says that loving God actively and being content go together, whereas loving money and being content do not. Whatever contentment looks like, it means to "*pursue* righteousness, godliness, faith, love, endurance and gentleness" (v. 11, italics mine). Contentment is not about being bland, lifeless, weak or passive.

THE STRENGTH HOPE PROVIDES

When Paul said, "These three remain: faith, hope and love. But the greatest of these is love" (1 Corinthians 13:13), he might just as well have added "and the least understood is hope." Yet we'd do well to study it, for contentment is a child of hope. If our future is secure, we rest in the present. We can live in the limitations of today when we know that things will work out tomorrow or eventually, in the thousand tomorrows of heaven.

What gives us this confidence? The writer of Hebrews puts it this way: "Be content with what you have, because God has said, 'Never will I leave you; never will I forsake you'" (13:5). Our circumstances can be endured because God is trustworthy; he will walk alongside us forever.

True hope liberates us from needing This Thing or This Event to be our momentary salvation. If we don't get what we want now, it's okay. Something better awaits. In addition, as Henri Nouwen says, "Hope frees us from the need to predict the future." Today we suffer the irony that the greater our affluence, the less trusting we seem to be. More begets the need for more. When I had five shirts, I laughed at the luxury of having thirty. Now that I have thirty, I find that I could use a few more.

Biblical hope is not "a belief in a positive outcome related to events and circumstances in one's life." Christ-defined hope is not defined by circumstances. It is not what we mean when we say "I hope the weather will be nice today," as if hope were mere wishful sentiment.

So, in one sense, worry and covetousness are both expressions of deficient hope. We lust when we don't trust. If the present is all in all, and we feel deprived or wounded in the present, we tend to compensate for our anxiety or boredom with food, busyness, flashy images or ever-present music. But when our hope is in something that transcends our circumstances, our circumstances cannot take away our hope. As Paul puts it, "I have learned the secret of being content in any and every situation, whether well fed or hungry, whether living in plenty or in want" (Philippians 4:12).

Our current times seem more noted for desperation than hope. For men, this lack of hope often translates into anger. Why are so many men consistently impatient, leaning on the hair trigger of their rage over every type of failure? How can these men be content when they feel urgent pressure to impress, to accumulate wealth, to be both aggressive and vulnerable, to be a good man in a world that presents so many confusing versions of that good man?

For many women, a lack of hope is expressed as excessive worry. Some women get stuck thinking that, no matter what they do, they have always disappointed someone. How can women be content when they feel the need to be objects of envy, to be powerful while appearing powerless, to be both sexy and modest, to be a good woman in a world that presents contradictory definitions of that good woman?

We all need the strength hope supplies. Our contentment depends on it.

A SATISFYING WAY

"What happened to my wonderful child?" This question is often raised by parents when their kids reach junior-high age. Like a werewolf before a rising moon, a contented kid transforms into a sullen monster. I overstate, but we can learn something about contentment by looking at younger children. They live for today, trust their parents to care for them and realize that success requires repeated effort.

Another resource, the Westminster Shorter Catechism, says that the satisfying way requires "full contentment with our own condition, with a right and charitable frame of spirit" toward our neighbors and all that is theirs. Our goal is a heartfelt appreciation for what we have and a generous approval that our neighbors have what they have.

If we keep in mind a few questions, we are more likely to maintain good perspective. I call the following a "contentment catechism."

Who am I? A child of the Father, a friend rescued by Jesus, a vessel alive in the Spirit. (1 John 3:1; 1 Peter 3:18; Romans 5:5)

What is important in life? Loving God and my neighbor. (Mark 12:28-31)

What can separate me from what is important? Nothing. (Romans 8)

What can I do to make things better? Work and give thanks. (Colossians 3:17)

What can I do about the things I can't control? Put hope in God. (Psalm 42:5)

During a time in my life of great pain and uncertainty, I profited from repeating these questions and answers. They reminded me of larger truths and reduced my anxiety. How can we consistently live this way? We have to die.

❦ THE DISCIPLINE OF *ARS MORENDI*

The Black Plague. Brutal war. High infant mortality. No antibiotics. Perhaps because death seemed to walk constantly with those in the Middle Ages, the church thought that believers needed to prepare to meet their Savior, to learn to "let go" of this life and die with grace. They called this practice *ars morendi*, Latin for "the art of dying well." As the discipline for contentment, it applies to more than getting ready for physical death. But so what? Who wants to study death? Our culture treats death in paradox. We are both attracted to death (as seen in our love for violence in the media) and distanced from death (as seen in our denial of aging and the placement of cemeteries away from daily view). Perhaps this old practice has something to teach us.

Ars morendi reminds us that no matter how our culture views death, we have some good dying to do. This may seem to contradict the admonition to "choose life," but it does not. Everybody dies. Choosing life does not mean that we ignore this fact. And everybody dies on the way to death; that is, everyone, on some level, dies to self. We have to die to laziness if we hope to accomplish anything at all. We have to die to certain foods if we want to be healthy. We have to die to the need to dominate if we are going to encourage others to flourish.

Dying well as good surrender. Spiritual submission is a redemptive form of giving in; it is a sacramental good acceptance. Thomas Merton says it well: "My chief care should not be to find pleasure or success, health or life or money or rest or even things like virtue and wisdom—still less their opposite, pain, failure, sickness, death. But in all that happens, my one desire and my one joy should be to know: 'Here is the thing that God has willed for me.'" A healthy acquiescence is part of *ars morendi*.

Surrendering to what "God has willed for me" is an acceptance that *this is my life*. Not my past. Not my future. *This* present, *this* life. *This* is my house, not the one my neighbor has. *This* is my spouse, not the one on TV or the Internet. *This* is the child I was given, the one with the strong will, the one with disease, the one with heartache. When I feel overwhelmed grading papers and exams, I try to remember, "*This* is the life I've chosen." Sometimes this one line settles me into a more contented state. Other times, nothing seems to help. But through it all, I want—at the very least—to be able to say, "*This* is the situation in which God is instructing me."

When we surrender to the life we've been given, we often relax and perform our tasks better. As jazz violinist Stephen Nachmanovitch says, we "play freely" when we have "nothing to gain and nothing to lose." If we think much is at stake, that "one mistake and I'm finished," we usually tighten up. Nachmanovitch says, "I am not in the music business; . . . I am in the surrender business. . . . Surrender means cultivating a comfortable attitude toward not knowing." Sounds a lot like faith and hope to me. We are more likely to be content when, instead of insisting that we win or meet our goals, we trust God for what we do not know.

Dying well via surrender also involves a form of detachment. Although the word *detachment* itself might be a little off-putting, the idea is as liberating as they come. Our tendency is to link our contentment to the *effects* of our actions. If contentment is dependent on our flawless piano recital or getting our coworkers' praise, our focus is on the *results* of our actions instead of on the actions themselves—and results are not in our control.

Detachment (freedom from obsessing over results) does not mean that we are callous about what happens. It means we are responsible for our choices, not the choices of others, for faithfulness, not for success. At my college, I teach as well as I can. Sometimes students respond well, and sometimes they don't. Of course, I do all I can to get them caught up in the beauty and usefulness of a new idea. But I am much more content when I concentrate on whether or not I have been faithful to the tasks I've been given, not whether Joe Schmoe is excited about his education. Joe has his own issues—and my teaching might not reach him in this moment.

Dying well as a "turning toward" and a "turning away from." Choosing one scene or word or attitude is dying to a different scene or word or attitude. Of course, sometimes we "die" in the wrong direction. When I turn my desires toward a woman in a bikini on the beach—often literally, but certainly symbolically—I am turning away from my wife. When I covet my neighbor's car, I am turning away from my own.

Sometimes the most important thing we can do is change the way we talk about something, to turn toward a new way of naming a situation. To call a slow-moving line in a grocery store "a tragedy" will yield more discontentment than to call it "an opportunity to relax." We often need to reframe. When I turn toward God as the source of my hope, I turn away from my self-centeredness. When I frame my goals as "seeking first his kingdom and his righteousness," I turn away from thinking that some trivial product will revolutionize my life.

Back to the theme of the road trip. As my entire family knows, I do not like to get lost while driving. Even though we have always eventually found our destination and nothing of importance has ever been jeopardized by our temporary misdirection, I hate turning around or going one mile too far. I fume. I raise my voice. I tell myself I am a failure.

Part of dealing with this failure has to do with how I talk about failure. Is getting lost a "giant failure" or a "tiny mistake"? And why do we say we are lost when we are only a street away from our destination? For me, the real failure is my reactionary impatience and disrespectful treatment of my family. I could just as easily have called the situation an adventure or a midterm exam in patience or an experiment in problem solving. These alternatives are not phony-baloney, pie-in-the-sky optimisms. On a practical level, I can accept getting off track when I work to reframe the situation more positively or modestly, when I die to certain ways of talking about it.

Jeremiah Burroughs saw the same need to change the way we talk about our suffering: A sinful heart thinks, "I must have my wants made up or else it is impossible that I should be content. But a gracious heart says, 'What is the duty of the circumstances God has put me into?'" To Burroughs, becoming like Jesus means, in part, transforming the way we interpret "God's actions" toward us. The way we think and talk drives our behavior. Or, to say it differently, the way we believe should influence the way we think and talk. Today we hear so many messages contrary to our faith that it should not surprise us that we have significant, steady reframing to do. Few tasks will influence our contentment more, because reframing is central to the good dying we are called to practice as part of *ars morendi*.

When a windstorm had blown down a neighbor's trellis, I mounted a ladder to fix the bougainvillea once more to the house. After reattaching the trellis, I held the heavy, resisting vine with one hand, careful not to grab any of its sharp, three-inch spikes, and I attempted to tie it up with wire. When I pressed the vine hard to the trellis, the bougainvillea slipped out of my hand and whipped violently against my face, smacking me in the eye. As I took stock of the injury, I kept envisioning a giant spike piercing my eye, maybe blinding me forever. Curiously, all I could think was that it hadn't happened. Ecstatic with joy, I could barely make my way off the ladder without falling.

Later came an even more curious consequence. For weeks, though my eyelid bore a bruise, I experienced more contentment than I had in years. Everything became a gift to me. The bougainvillea smacked me into reframing, with gratitude and faith the result.

To live the unsatisfied life in a satisfying way requires that we die, that we practice *ars morendi*. As we surrender and reframe, we conform our hearts to the heart of Jesus and learn to see our circumstances and ourselves as the Father sees us, as his children, as his beloved, as receivers of gifts piled higher than any Christmas haul. This is why Jesus ends the Matthew passage with "seek first his kingdom and his righteousness, and all these things will be given to you as well" (6:33). It is the way to contentment. Thankfully, his kingdom is not outside ourselves, in circumstances we mistakenly think we can control. The kingdom of God is within us (Luke 17:21).

That, I believe, we could safely call good news.

FOR DISCUSSION OR REFLECTION

1. Jesus says, "Where your treasure is, there your heart will be also" (Matthew 6:21). What is your treasure? Another way to ask this is, "What do you spend your time desiring?" If someone listened to you talk over a long period of time, what would they say you *want?* What desires do you talk about?

2. All discontentment might come down to one word: *if.* What future events does your contentment depend on?

3. What are your thoughts about your "totalitarian impulse," your innate desire to control? In what areas of your life do you see this impulse becoming destructive? How have you managed to control your desire for control?

4. Some have said that recent generations are marked by a sense of entitlement. To whatever degree this is true for you, how do you see deservedness influencing your sense of contentment? About what kinds of things are you typically grateful and typically ungrateful? How do you account for the difference?

5. Have you ever been content? When? Why?

6. Consider the definition offered: Contentment is the strength hope gives us to pursue the unsatisfied life in a satisfying way. Is that definition satisfying? Why or why not?

EXERCISE

1. List your top five worries. Share an experience in which the idea "*this* is my life" made a difference in your worry, when you consciously surrendered to your present circumstances.

2. In the spirit of Christ's call for us to die to ourselves and our sin (Luke 9:23), consider a few small things you could die to. One way to do this is to commit with a friend to practice a "Lenten daily." Deny yourself one small thing every day for a week (such as dessert, TV, e-mail), then discuss with a friend how this has influenced your contentment.

3. Look back at your list of your top five worries. State each one as you usually do, then reframe the line, phrasing it in a way that you think is more consistent with the life of Jesus.

8 ❧ GENEROSITY

fingers, fists and an open hand

The quality of mercy is not strain'd,

It droppeth as the gentle rain from heaven

Upon the place beneath: it is twice blest;

It blesseth him that gives and him that takes.

WILLIAM SHAKESPEARE

We saw the fire for the first time when we drove over a rise near our house. Fanned by seventy-mile-an-hour winds, the flames exploded down a hillside. Terrified, we raced home and grabbed what we could in twenty minutes, our hearts pounding and eyes wide in disbelief. As embers swept under eaves and into attics, over two hundred houses burned in about eight hours, including fourteen in our immediate neighborhood.

The Chinese name their years. They called a recent one the Year of the Rat and another the Year of the Ox. For us, the last twelve months could be called the Year of the Panic Attack.

In addition to the fire disaster, the economy crumbled. Real-estate prices plunged and stores closed. After my brother lost his job, he met with the president of a large chamber of commerce, who told him, "You'll never work again." Duly depressed, he and his wife tightened their belts.

These days, we hear a lot about holding on to what we've got, squeezing what we can out of the little money or time we have left. Maybe we should call this the Year of the Clenched Fist, the year of hunkering down, tightening up, pulling back, of grabbing and gripping. These are times when clenching makes sense. But here, as in so many areas, Jesus turns our thinking upside-down:

> Bless those who curse you, pray for those who mistreat you. If someone slaps you on one cheek, turn the other also. If someone takes your coat, do not withhold your shirt. . . . But love your enemies, do good to them, and lend to them without expecting to get anything back. . . . Forgive, and you will be forgiven. Give, and it will be given to you. (Luke 6:28-29, 35, 37-38)

Jesus says that when times are bad, when people misunderstand us, when they hate us enough to cuss us out and treat us poorly, here's what we should do: love. And when it's plenty cold outside and someone wants our windbreaker, we should give it up, and our shirt if need be. In tough times, when we feel abused and put-upon, Jesus says to lend and give and love and forgive. He says, "Open your hand, be generous."

Though we may not recently have been directly cursed or asked for the shirt off our back, we know what Jesus means. Generosity is a way of relating to others that is not dependent on circumstances. Victims of the massive Santa Barbara Tea Fire were said to have "lost everything." But the "burned out" did not talk this way. Yes, they lost prized heirlooms. They grieved over personal papers consumed by flames, and autographed books, and musical instruments. But they talked about still having their lives, the love of God and the support of friends. They had lost a house but not a home, photographs but not memories, place settings but not the ability to host a feast. They lost possessions but they talked generously.

In fact, all that is necessary for generosity to function is some-one who wants or needs something from us. We need never fear there will be a shortage in this area. So we don't have to store up two weeks of free time or a completed to-do list before we give an hour to someone. We don't need five hundred pounds of self-esteem before we praise others or listen to them well. Generosity is more like a river than a lake. It's the flowing that matters, not the storage. Circumstances don't dictate generosity. We do.

GENEROSITY WITH PALMS UP

As I mentioned earlier, my mother-in-law, Connie, has Alzheim-er's. When she first started to show signs of dementia, the dearest grandma our girls could ever hope for occasionally said mean things and took to hitting when she didn't like what was happen-ing to her. At our dinner table, she once said that I should be thrown in the trash.

In response to these and other losses, my wife, Janet, has been my teacher. Simply put, I have been flabbergasted by Janet's gener-osity, overwhelmed by her patience and tenderness. She smiled through the verbal attacks from her mom, tended gently to her needs (many of which were quite unpleasant) and always, always, always, expressed her affection.

And even now, though Connie has declined such that she is al-most wordless and expressionless, not knowing who we are and not even looking up when we arrive, Janet goes to her mother with open hands. "It's me, Mom, your daughter, Janet." The tears come before or after—but when we are there, Janet takes Connie's hands and holds them as if she could pass health and life and love right through them into Connie's being. And maybe she does. She always ends with "I love you" and a sweet kiss on her mother's cheek.

I tell you this story because you will see Janet's character all over my definition: generosity is *the predisposition to love open-handedly*. Our hands matter, both literally and symbolically. In the open hand, our palms are up and our fingers extended. A closed hand is usually a clenched fist, tightly grasping what it wants to keep or tensely preparing for battle. To be generous requires that we open our hands.

By word association, I leap from open palms to Palm Sunday, the beginning of Holy Week. After this event comes the clenched fists of the mob, clamoring for Jesus' death over Barabbas's. Eventually, Jesus opens his arms in crucifixion, suffering unto death. Here we see generosity in the flesh—an openhandedness that took a nail on our behalf.

Fingers extended. Our dog, Mocha, a fifty-pound mutt, has a secret handshake. Though she is more harmless than a dust bunny (we call her the scaredy-dog—as opposed to the scaredy-cat), she has a big bark. If visitors approach her by extending the back of their hands, Mocha keeps barking, or at least continues to act with suspicion. But if strangers reach an open hand toward Mocha, she apparently decides—for reasons unknown to us—that all is well. She relaxes, allows herself to be petted and actually stands guard next to the visitor.

All who open their hands toward Mocha make themselves vulnerable, more at risk to be chomped. It's a calculated choice, based in part on trusting Mocha's wagging tail and our words that "she won't hurt you." Extending one's fingers in a generous gesture always requires trust that the open hand will not be met with meat-munching canines or, more broadly, that what is given will be accepted and can be replenished. And this is not to say that we aren't sometimes punished for being generous. It *is* risky, but not to take the risk is to deny the chief purpose of a hand.

Designed to give. Sometimes, in a rare feat of athletic skill, I think, *Wow, so that's what the human body can do.* And sometimes, when I teach, I think, *This feels so right; it's what I was made for.* Likewise I believe the human soul has been designed for generosity. It is our operating system, our food, our fulfillment, our joy. It's not just our self at its best; it's how the self was created to function. At times, during the postfire trauma, I thought, *I can't wait until this period passes and I find myself grateful and generous again.* But this sentiment is wrong-headed. Generosity is not an *end* toward which we are moving; it is a *means.* Without generosity, our soul diminishes, like a body without exercise, sustenance and sleep. Brain chemistry goes screwy. Our whole life breaks down.

Yet this giving-out action can seem counterintuitive. When we are feeling weak, we can't imagine being generous. We "know" we will be depleted for extending ourselves. But the remarkable truth about loving others is that love, the parent virtue of generosity, is a resource that does not diminish when used. Love is not in a storage tank that gets drawn upon and then used up until someone loves us in return, putting fuel back in the tank. Love is exactly the opposite; it grows through generosity.

Lewis Hyde explains this regenerating phenomenon in his fascinating book *The Gift: Imagination and the Erotic Life of Property.* He's talking about romantic love in the subtitle: "To speak of gifts that survive their use is to describe a natural fact: libido is not lost when it is given away. Eros never wastes his lovers." When we feel "in love," we are not exhausted for expressing our romantic feelings or serving our beloved. Instead, we are energized—even while we are expending energy—and I believe all good love works this way. Thomas Merton echoes this idea in a chapter title: "Love Can Be Kept Only by Being Given Away." He says that the best love "increases in proportion as it is shared." Generosity does not deplete us; it feeds us.

Of course, if you give away a mango, you have one less mango, but think of the times you have planned and carried out a loving act, a truly generous gesture. My guess is that the more effort you put into the gift, the less depleting the act felt. You might have felt physically tired after digging a ditch for a friend, but you were probably also exhilarated.

THE CLENCHED FIST

Other than for holding on to things, a clenched fist seems best suited for a fight. When walking with my girls in San Francisco a few years ago, a drugged-out man leaped in front of them and said a few nasty things. I didn't realize at the time, but my wife told me later that I thrust my chest out and clenched my fists. I was ready to pound this guy into a heap of mush—me, a guy who has *never* been in a fistfight!

When threatened, our instinct is to clench. Under stress, we often tighten our neck or abdominal muscles. At night, many of us clench our jaw, for which we suffer the next day. Clenching comes naturally; it's unclenching that takes training. We pay good money for relaxation seminars, yoga sessions and massage therapy, learning all manner of destressing techniques. No one goes to a conference titled "The Top Ten Ways to Make Your Neck Immobile."

Just as the open hand tells us something about being generous, the closed hand tells us something about being stingy. In fact, generosity is so naturally connected to the hand that we call a financially ungenerous person "tightfisted." A clenched fist has many limitations. We may be able to keep what we are grasping, but we can't add anything to it, nor can we accept something into our palm.

Until I was nearly fourteen, I was the shortest, skinniest kid in my grade. That's one reason for the lack of fistfights. As the picked-on pipsqueak, I clenched my fists a lot, in fear and disappointment, like when Jennifer said, "Never dance with Greg. He's so short!" We may clench for understandable reasons, from childhood inadequacies to adult anxiety, but these explanations do not keep the clenching from having its harmful effect on us.

Clenching the miserly way. Sometimes we clench out of fear of what we might lose. We see "what we possess" as a zero-sum proposition. If we subtract from our bank account, we have less in our bank account. End of discussion. This fear can lead us to believe that we *never* have enough. Our sense of being loved is not full enough for us to extend hospitality to others. Our stockpile of compliments received needs to be higher before we can offer encouragement.

Sometimes I really *do* have too much to lose. But most of the time, I am just insecure, or I hold on to a grudge because I worry that if I let go, the other person won't get the justice of my anger. I hold my possessions close because I fear that my power tools or my car will get ruined by careless borrowers. But a generous heart knows that "too much to lose" is a losing proposition, that holding too tightly changes us; it turns us into clinging creatures, weaker, more deprived, bound by chains to things, less able to travel lightly, the way good pilgrim-disciples do.

Clenching the gluttonous way. Sometimes we clench out of greed for what we might gain. We see a lavish lifestyle as our birthright, and we promise we'll be bighearted beyond belief just as soon as we win the lottery. Gluttony doesn't always take obvious forms, as if the greedy are all country-club socialites thumbing their noses from their Ferraris. Children show greed when they say, "I just *have to have*" the most popular jacket or the latest technological thing. We adults are less shameless, but we often believe the lie that a new sweater or a better friend or a higher-status job will solve our problems. A generous heart knows that a clenching greediness turns us into gobbling creatures who grasp after everything but are never satisfied, who devour praise and profits but always demand more. Greed believes that "getting stuff" will accomplish what only God can accomplish, that is, satisfy the deepest longings of a wounded heart.

THE OPEN HAND

When we returned to our house after the fire, we stood dumbfounded as we saw the burn spots on our house and three of the homes that encircle ours smoldering in ashes, copper pipes bent over, appliances standing out in the open like rusty cans. I'd never been so exhausted and tense at the same time as I was in the weeks that followed.

Open hands came immediately, offering sandwiches and clothes, temporary housing and money. People begged to help: "Can I walk your dog, make pancakes, watch kids, repair windows, clean up the yard or search through the rubble?" And those whose houses burned down displayed generosity beyond comprehension. One told other faculty members to "step up" and be the leaders we needed to be. Others said, "Well, we've wanted to live more simply. I guess we are on our way."

Generosity is the extension of an open hand. Literally. At a four-way stop, when we might compete for our right to go first, we can motion with our hand for the other to go. When someone wants to borrow clothing or a vase, we can move toward our possession with an open hand. If others need some time to talk, we can gesture to an empty seat with an open hand. When God calls us, we could pray with open hands. It's a physical and spiritual fact. We can't hold on and let go at the same time.

A PREDISPOSITION TO LOVE

When we hear that love conquers all, we sometimes feel inspired, and we tell our brain to send the message to open our hands. We want to be the type of generous person who is predisposed to be generous, someone who is inclined in the direction of others and their needs. If "God loves a cheerful giver" (2 Corinthians 9:7), he might not be enthusiastic about a crabby one. Like all the virtues, generosity is meant to come from the heart, to be a desire and a joy, not just a duty.

But you say, "I wish this were the case. More often than not, I have to make myself be generous." That's okay. Welcome to the task of daily life. Even so, we're better off with a vision for where we are headed. The goal of a predisposition to love openhandedly keeps us moving toward the most thoroughgoing kind of generosity. By God's grace, we are not just becoming people who act generously but we are becoming generous people. We are becoming predisposed to love, to give, to raise the question of loving well before we ask, "What's in it for me?" or "How will I be inconvenienced?"

And this is the thing about love; there is no act good enough to be truly admirable without it. Not pedaling in a bike race to raise awareness about cancer, not helping a neighbor stake a tree in the wind and rain when your favorite sporting event is on television. Don't get me wrong; it's not bad to do good things—the hungry need food and will enjoy whatever sustenance we provide—but if we offer the spoon without love, we "gain nothing," as Paul says (1 Corinthians 13:3). Love is needed for generosity to be as good as it can be. Merton puts it simply but beautifully: "If we are going to love others at all, we must make up our minds to love them well." Generosity involves loving fully, richly, deeply. So, what does "loving well" look like? How is it related to generosity?

Loving well by keeping gifts in motion. In *The Gift*, Hyde recounts the story of how the Massim people in the South Sea Islands make gifts (such as necklaces) and then row canoes over to a neighboring island to deliver their gifts. Members of the receiving tribe then make their own gifts and row over to a *different* island—and the pattern continues. Eventually, the first gift-givers receive something from yet another tribe, but they have no control over how well it matches the worth of the original gift. According to Hyde, who sees this same pattern in many Western folk tales also, the key is that gifts must be kept in motion: "Each gift stays with a man for a while, but if he keeps it too long he will begin to have a reputation for being 'slow' and 'hard.'" In the gift economy, the norm is to give.

Contrary to our norm of mutual reciprocity (exchanging goods in a "this for that" sort of way), Hyde says that many groups around the globe practice circular reciprocity, setting gifts in motion without knowing how they might eventually be compensated. True generosity is closer to the gift economy than it is to the market economy, because it lets go and trusts God to complete the circle. For all the benefits of capitalism, it has a way of creeping into places it does not belong. When we "invest" in people, we expect a dividend. Our generosity can be corrupted by a watchful spirit of compensation. We ask friends to dinner but are upset when they do not reciprocate. We skip some work to talk to someone who is troubled, and we think God should supernaturally whisk the work away. We tithe to the church and expect spiritual blessings in exchange.

How wonderful it would be if the "gift in motion" mentality could improve our desire to pass on the level of generosity extended to us. Someone brings flowers when they visit us, so we take a book to the next person who hosts us. Unexpectedly, a superficial conversation turns into a deep and meaningful one, so we decide to initiate prayer in our next conversation. When we need help—financial or emotional—gifts of support arrive, so we find the time to help paint a house or make dinner for an inner-city ministry. We keep gifts in motion, living out the expansive nature of generosity. Eugene Peterson's version of Proverbs 11:24 puts it this way: "The world of the generous gets larger and larger; the world of the stingy gets smaller and smaller" (*The Message*). We are not made less by giving; we are made more.

Loving as your neighbor loves to be loved. During my first year of marriage, I learned that if Janet felt sad, I could bring a smile to her face by playing one of her favorite musicals and giving her a hug. During the same year of marriage, Janet learned that if I felt depressed, I was not about to be cheered up by *The Sound of Music* or *My Fair Lady*. Although I have learned to enjoy musicals (well, many of them), the operating principle of love has not changed: the receiver of love is the one who decides if the generous gesture feels generous.

The beloved determines whether the gift is, indeed, a loving act. This is what "love your neighbor as yourself" is all about. It means to love your neighbor as you love to be loved—and you love to be loved according to your own idiosyncratic tastes and needs. Let's suppose I love peanut butter (which I do). For me to give peanut butter to a hungry child because I love peanut butter is not a loving act if the hungry child is allergic to peanut butter. I am not being generous because I give to others what *I* find loving. I am generous if I give to others what *they* find loving. You might say, "Isn't it the thought that counts?" I say, "Only if the recipient decides to think in those terms." Thankfully, those we attempt to love often do.

To love openhandedly is to love well, to give wholeheartedly by keeping gifts in motion and loving our neighbors as they want and need to be loved. The most generous of all gestures, selfless choices, confound contemporary sociobiologists such as Sigmund, Fehr and Nowak: "The prevalence of altruistic acts—providing benefits to a recipient at a cost to the donor—can seem hard to reconcile with the idea of the selfish gene, the notion that evolution at its base acts solely to promote genes that are adept at engineering their own proliferation." When evolution *must* account for all our behaviors, generosity makes that accounting difficult.

GENEROSITIES APLENTY

The idea of generosity typically sends us to thoughts about money. And money does matter. Scriptures addressing our financial decisions are numerous, including the following:

> The wicked borrow and do not repay, but the righteous give generously. (Psalm 37:21)

> No one can serve two masters. Either you will hate the one and love the other, or you will be devoted to the one and despise the other. You cannot serve both God and Money. (Matthew 6:24)

But to our detriment, we both overstate and understate the connection between generosity and money. We overstate it by reducing generosity to tithing, so we neglect other aspects of generosity. We understate it by denying the link between generosity and money as a test of other aspects of our generosity. Though most of the words for being ungenerous are tied to finances (being miserly, stingy, tightfisted), penny pinching goes way beyond what we do with our money. We can be miserly with our praise, stingy with our time and tightfisted with our forgiveness. Generosity needs to be seen broadly.

Generosity of spirit: Spontaneous yes-ness. In his book on improvisational theater, Keith Johnstone says that a spirit of acceptance is at the core of good ad-libbing. He differentiates between actors who generously accept what other actors introduce into a scene and those who consistently resist:

> There are people who prefer to say "Yes," and there are people who prefer to say "No." Those who say "Yes" are rewarded by the adventures they have, and those who say "No" are rewarded by the safety they attain. There are far more "No" sayers around than "Yes" sayers, *but you can train one type to behave like the other.*

Improv works when the actor who says, "Please take the fish I have here in this paper bag," is answered with, "I'd love to. I'll walk it all the way to Argentina." The spirit of acceptance that is central to the stage is also important in the drama of living.

I like to think about generosity of spirit as the spontaneous preference for yes-ness. When a need is presented, the first response from the person whose spirit is generous is yes. This person may not always provide what is requested, but the desire, the predisposition, is evident. "Yes, you can borrow my car." "Yes, I can meet with you."

Too often our first reaction is no. We naysay because we are worried about the consequences of being generous. We don't want to feel out of control of our resources. Some suppress spontaneous yes-ness until, by force of habit, a huge wall of no-ness has to be surmounted for them to get to yes. Of course, some say yes too often. To be generous does not mean to have no boundaries, as if generosity is an absolute, an idol that requires us to sacrifice marriage, family and health on its bloody altar.

As frightening as spontaneous yes-ness sometimes feels, we can learn to be more generous-minded and generous-hearted. Generous-mindedness means to give others the benefit of the doubt. It says, "Yes, I will resist judgment until all of the evidence is in." It means recognizing that the person who cut in front of you in the grocery store may be rushing to get home due to an emergency. Maybe the person criticizing you suffers from enormous insecurities. Generous-mindedness also means respecting the truth in every remark and valuing the person who speaks that truth. After hearing a condemning comment during a debate, Yale philosopher Nicholas Wolterstorff said, "We should always disagree with our opponents, even historical figures, as if they were in the room with us. Would we ridicule Darwin or Freud if they were in our presence?"

Generous-heartedness relates to emotional giving, the ways we "rejoice with those who rejoice" and "mourn with those who mourn" (Romans 12:15). Can we be happy when *others* receive awards *we* had hoped for? Can we be sympathetic when an enemy encounters loss? No doubt the most significant expression of generous-heartedness is saying yes to forgiveness. Would we be able to forgive a person who publicly exposed a weakness of ours? When we forgive, are we quick to forgive? And can we forgive ourselves for the stupid thing we said, the remark that wounded a child or turned a friend away from us? Generosity of heart, as heard in the voice of forgiveness, is one of the miracles of humanity. That it happens as often as it does speaks to God's mercy at work in the world.

Generosity of spirit applies to the world of competition. It certainly connects to my tennis game, especially when I make difficult line calls. I "call 'em as I see 'em," but I see 'em in my favor more often than I should. When I'm not sure that the ball is out, am I generous enough to rule in my opponent's favor? Well, sometimes. I'm working on it. In a redemptive way, generosity permits what we might call a holy competition, an attempt to "be the best" at serving others. Some of the time, competition brings out the worst in us, but when we try to "win the contest" of being generous, each generous act inspires a more generous act, until an irrepressible joy overtakes us.

We know what generosity of spirit looks like. It is the mercy motive that moves us to open our hands. It is generosity in its highest form, a mindful and heartfelt predisposition to love.

Generosity of speech: Praise without flattery. Most of us can easily recall a verbal bullet that pierced our soul and lodged in our memory. ("You are stupid. You won't amount to anything.") We can also remember the actions that encouraged us toward greater accomplishment. Someone came alongside us and said we had a gift for science or music or listening well. Generosity of speech has to do with making word decisions for the sake of constructive support. Not all praise builds up and not all ridicule tears down, but we can see the effect of influential words when we examine our experience.

So, how can we bless others with our speech? Skillful praise matters. Flattery is the praise of others for our sake; it is an attempt to manipulate others by exaggerating the worth of their deeds. But generous praise, especially when it is personal and detailed, has the power to "render the unspeakable speakable" (as Walker Percy puts it), to name a person's qualities in memorable, life-changing ways.

My English professor when I was a college freshman usually flopped into class a few minutes late, tossed books across the front table and onto the floor, and began his lecture mid-sentence, as if we had all been in the hallway listening to his introductory remarks. This endearingly eccentric man welcomed me into his office to chat about my poetry. Almost forty years later, his angel-voice of encouragement still rises against the demon voices telling me I should not bother to work with words at all.

On the other hand, we've all been around people whose minds are elsewhere when we are talking; they're planning the next event or thinking about the person they really want to be with. This experience reminds us that listening well is perhaps the highest form of conversational generosity. Attending to another's story, asking questions and letting others vent can encourage as much as any list of compliments. Although Jesus was talking about parables when he said, "If anyone has ears to hear, let them hear" (Mark 4:23), the statement is rich for many uses of our ears. Next Jesus explains, "Consider carefully what you hear. . . . With the measure you use, it will be measured to you—and even more" (v. 24). Good listening not only blesses the speaker, it makes the listener more receptive. Listening wholeheartedly requires that we relinquish our power to be unmoved.

Generosity of time: A way to think about patience. One of the louder virtues in American culture is efficiency. It's what makes the clock of capitalism tick. We are remarkably skilled at getting things done, at thinking "yes, we can" and then putting forth our best effort to accomplish many tasks in a short time. Often efficiency serves us well. But this way of valuing time can tick-tock into our worldview, leading us to measure everything by the stopwatch. Time: we march against it, beat it, save it, manage it, spend it, and try not to kill it or waste it. If efficiency becomes a dictator instead of a servant, generosity is usually oppressed. We feel we must fill all days with industrious busyness.

When my daughters were young, I too frequently bemoaned how little time I could give to writing. One friend said, "Your girls will only be toddlers once. Don't worry so much about being productive." Another friend gestured to my daughters and said, "Spence, *here* are your publications!" These friends encouraged me to view time in a *kairos* perspective, time by the opportunity presented, time according to what the season calls for. Time well used, by a *kairos* standard, is time that appropriately meets the needs of the moment, not a *chronos* standard, time measured by the demands of the clock.

For the most part, the test of the generosity of time is patience. When it comes to time, can I extend the open hand? Don't get me wrong; *chronos* and efficiency have their place. But most of my impatience is not an expression of my commitment to good time management. I just want things done now, on my terms. A more generous relationship to time says, "I wait for the LORD, my whole being waits, and in his word I put my hope" (Psalm 130:5).

Generosity of possessions: To have and not to hold. Seeing this heading, you might be thinking, *I don't mind reading about generosity of spirit and time and speech, even of physical sacrifice, but, hey, my stuff is my stuff.* Indeed. If I call my possessions "mine, all mine," I will mainly want to protect them, hoard them or show them off. My attitude would change significantly if I said that my possessions were "material gifts God put into my palm to care for and offer to others." I might then more freely lend underlined books or prized dishes and not worry about what happens to them.

Word choice regarding possessions gets more complicated, according to Luke Johnson, because of current uses of the English language. The problem, he says, is the word *have*. We say both "I have an arm" and "I have a car," though the first "have" relates to being and the second "have" relates to ownership. Because we use the word *have* in relationship to our identity, we can easily think that when we use the word in reference to our belongings, we are making a statement about who we are.

Often these choices are innocuous: books on our shelves that represent our interests, a style of clothing that is consistent with our personality or a funny saying on a coffee mug. But sometimes more is at stake. Johnson puts it this way,

> Every claim of ownership, therefore, involves an ambiguity; we say, this is *mine*, but we imply as well, this is *me*. . . . The real difficulty regarding possessions lies in what they mean to us. The real mystery concerning possessions is how they relate to our sense of identity and worth as human beings. The real sin related to possessions has to do with the willful confusion of being and having.

When I want others to see my possessions as "me," I am declaring that my worth is found in what I own, not in God's view of me. But when I stop thinking of my tools and clothes and car and house as physical extensions of me, I can let them go. I am not relinquishing part of my identity; I am only letting material objects go through my hands. As a psalmist says, "Good will come to those who are generous and lend freely, who conduct their affairs with justice" (Psalm 112:5).

Years ago, when our third daughter was born, we had to sell our smaller sporty wagon and get a car large enough for three car seats. Fifty-two inches wide across the back seat, to be precise. We ended up with a Fat American Cruiser, a giant older Buick the color of a tank. I was mortified. The Buick was neither a cool foreign car nor a funky American car. Since I saw my car as an extension of my identity, I didn't like the conclusions others might draw. But whenever I managed to see my identity as a child of God "in Christ" (Galatians 3:26), I could be more lighthearted about my possessions. We are not what we own.

Generosity of home: From open hand to open door. When my grandpa told me he was lonely living in his mobile home, I asked him if he ever invited neighbors over. He announced firmly, "I am not about to invite someone to my place until they have invited me to their place first." By that logic, of course, no one would ever invite anyone over.

In our times, hospitality appears to be a fading art. The generous act of welcoming others into our space is often crowded out by fatigue, an exaggerated sense of privacy and worry about what visitors will see. I am convinced that—as much as anything—embarrassment over our clutter and dust keeps us from caring for each other around the table.

Hospitality is the generosity of the open door. It includes all the ways we welcome others, from embracing an interruption wholeheartedly to inviting a stranded motorist to our house to spend the night. But hospitality is not just about the invitation; it is also about the way we say "welcome" after we open our doors. As Henri Nouwen says, "Hospitality . . . requires that the host feel at home in his own house and . . . that he create a free and fearless place for the unexpected visitor. . . . Hospitality is the ability to pay attention to the guest." The test of hospitality is not how often we "entertain," but how visitors respond in our presence.

Some may protest, "Isn't hospitality mainly for extroverts, those who are gifted for this work?" Indeed, hospitality is easier for some than others. But isn't this also true for bravery and self-control? The writer of Hebrews says, "Do not forget to show hospitality to strangers, for by so doing some people have shown hospitality to angels without knowing it" (13:2). Our sense of others' greater giftedness need not keep us from welcoming angels.

As the Tea Fire raged outside, Janet and I frantically packed up our two cars. Then the phone rang. Friends from church asked us if we needed a place to stay. What a relief to receive that call! How welcoming! Every day of the two weeks we were in their house, they seemed delighted to have us, even our animals. They opened their doors to us—and we fell into their arms, frightened but grateful. They showed us true hospitality.

Generosity of receiving: It's also a good thing. As we've heard a zillion times from our parents, "It is more blessed to give than to receive" (Acts 20:35)—in part because the givers get to watch what happens to receivers when they receive a gift. But receiving is blessed as well, not just because of how fun it is to receive, but because receivers get to watch what happens to givers when they give. If we refused all gifts, givers wouldn't be transformed by their acts of generosity.

Because of the fire in our area, a classroom of local third-graders sent a letter saying they wanted to give us food. We were touched by their sentiment but didn't need food, so we told the teacher that we had been displaced but we were doing fine. We said, "Check in with those who lost their homes." The teacher replied, "This is what *everyone* up here has said. These kids are desperate to help." So we said we would receive. They came to the door with giant smiles. Why should we deny third-graders the blessing of giving?

It's pride that usually keeps us from receiving. We don't want to feel beholden to others, to be in others' debt because they have given to us. We don't want to appear needy. Receiving moves us out of a position of control. It also requires an open hand.

Generosity of finances: Right on the money. You should know by now that you don't have to worry: This chapter is not primarily about your checkbook and credit cards. And, when you get to the end, I won't ask you to call a toll-free number to make a contribution, a dollar for each page you've finished.

But I do want to say that if generosity is not dependent on circumstances, generosity of finances is not dependent on how much money we have in the bank. Jesus affirms this principle when he praises the poor widow who contributes less than a penny to the offering (Mark 12:41-43). Sometimes I worry that when our kids rank our top ten sayings, "We can't afford it" will be on the list. That line can be a statement of fact, but it can also be an attitude of withholding, a spirit of restriction. If we are stingy, no amount of money will turn us into philanthropists.

Yet stinginess should not be confused with frugality, which is, in fact, the life-giving flip side of generosity. Those who are generous, Bernard Häring says, "keep discovering what they can do without," because they want to have more to give. Frugality is part of the technique of generosity. If I can save funds here, I can give it there. If I can be more resourceful with my time here, I can be more liberal with it there.

Our use of money says as much about our faith as anything. Do we trust God enough to loosen up our wallets? What would "spontaneous yes-ness" be without a readiness to say yes with our money? Doesn't generosity of time sometimes cost us personal income? Can we give of our home—our pantry and bedrooms—without holding our possessions lightly? As we move from the clenched fist to the open hand, we will decreasingly notice what we are giving up. Like the woman who poured expensive perfume on the head of Jesus (Matthew 26:6-13), we will be looking for the right moment to give away what we have.

✤ THE DISCIPLINE OF COMPASSIONATE IMAGINATION

The night of the fire, after we couldn't take any more TV news rehashing the same information with the same video, Janet and I went to bed. We didn't sleep much. We talked and wept and prayed. We imagined our house burning down. Surely it would be the first to go, because of the trees in front. All our possessions would be smoke and ashes. We pictured our lives starting over as homeless survivors.

By early morning, we learned which houses went down—and we talked and wept and prayed again. When we got up to the neighborhood, a quick and earnest empathy surged through all of us there, a deep sorrow for our friends whose houses burned. For all our human weakness, we know how to reach into the river of compassion that flows through us. When times are easy, we too often leave its banks, but we rush back to the sweet water when the suffering comes. It's the image of God in us.

We also discovered a simple appreciation that put possessions in perspective. We were all alive and unhurt. If the fire had occurred in the middle of the night, hundreds would have perished. And, as we cleaned up our own place, we kept saying, "Well, this could have burned." The phrase made it easier to let things go, to give away what remained. A compassionate imagination encourages empathy and appreciation, qualities that are central to the flourishing of generosity.

Compassionate imagination and empathy. Most of the time, generosity flows unrestrained toward friends, those whose circumstances mirror ours. In point of fact, I have never turned away a starving neighbor who has appeared on my doorstep. Of course, no starving neighbor has ever appeared there, because none of my neighbors are starving. Although we find it fairly easy to empathize with those who are similar to us, the hard thing is to love the neighbors who are not like us or who don't share our sidewalk.

I am convinced that one of God's purposes for the imagination is to deepen our empathy, to extend our compassion toward everyone, even our enemies. When we see their pain, we can imagine their loss, dwell in it, become like them as best we can. Isn't this part of the glory of the incarnation? Jesus left his place next to the Father and became like us. For our sake, he became a body that experienced hunger and weariness. He did not become a rock or celestial fireworks, but a person. The writer of Hebrews says, "For we do not have a high priest who is unable to empathize with our weaknesses, but we have one who has been tempted in every way, just as we are—yet he did not sin" (4:15). Amazingly, when Paul describes the incarnation, he says that, in our relationships with one another, we can have the same attitude of mind Christ Jesus had (Philippians 2:5).

We can have an incarnational attitude, a deep empathy, as we engage our imagination in spiritual service. G. K. Chesterton illustrates this activity as he shows how one of his characters, Detective Father Brown, is able to solve baffling crimes:

> I don't try to get outside the man. I try to get inside the murderer. . . . Indeed it's much more than that, don't you see? I *am* inside a man. I am always inside a man, moving his arms and legs; but I wait till I know I am inside a murderer, thinking his thoughts, wrestling with his passions. . . . Till I am really a murderer. . . . Yes, . . . that is what I call a religious exercise.

The call to generosity does not usually involve solving murders. But we can engage in a "religious exercise," a kind of spiritual speculation so that we feel what others are going through—from the inside. We might close our eyes and picture living in another person's circumstances, finding in ourselves the emotion and reason, the images and sounds associated with what others have experienced. We could study others' ways of being and even live among them or dress as they do.

Though my three children are unlike me in that they are female, I have tried to imagine their experiences—and I have learned much along the way: what it might be like to hear offensive, lewd comments or to be ignored because "girls don't care about such things." We can work to empathize with all humans as we delve deeply into our own humanity. As we become like our neighbors, we will know how to love them generously.

Compassionate imagination and appreciation. This discipline for generosity depends on the kind of gratitude that grows when we see what we have as bountiful. If what I have is more than I deserve, why should I be reluctant to give it away? Annie Dillard describes how we get to this place: "The world is fairly studded and strewn with pennies cast broadside by a generous hand. . . . But if you cultivate a healthy poverty and simplicity, so that finding a penny will literally make your day, then, since the world is in fact planted in pennies, you have with your poverty bought a lifetime of days." When all food is seen as a surprising mercy, we will say, "Have a bite of this peach. It is delicious." If we imagine a world deprived of the sun, we will say, "Come see this amazing sunset. Isn't it glorious?" Appreciation leads to generosity.

When we have less, or imagine having less, we often find how well we get along without our precious things. During my first sabbatical, we traveled across the country to Washington, D.C., for three months. All our possessions for that time fit into the trunk of our car. What freedom this poverty brought! How much we appreciated what came our way! Living with less helped loosen our ties to what we had.

Compassionate imagination is a discipline. Though it might be inevitable in the midst of a tragedy, we can develop it consciously.

When a person we dislike is hurting, we can empathetically imagine the pain. We can imitate the attitude of Jesus in his incarnation. And in a healthy poverty, we can picture our lives as a bounty of delights, appreciating the smile of a stranger and every ounce of rich, dark chocolate. It could all be gone tomorrow. Compassionate imagination moves us to be generous, to see our experience as grace, all grace. We do well to remember the words of Jesus: "Give, and it will be given to you. A good measure, pressed down, shaken together and running over, will be poured into your lap. For with the measure you use, it will be measured to you" (Luke 6:38).

FOR DISCUSSION OR REFLECTION

1. Discuss various associations you have with the words *giving* and *generosity*. How might the giving of money be or not be the truest test of generosity?

2. Given the definition of generosity (the predisposition to love openhandedly), what stories come to mind that show this virtue at work? Do these stories affirm or challenge the idea that love is not "used up" in generous actions?

3. Are you more likely to keep your fist clenched out of fear of losing or out of greed for what you might gain? Why? Provide examples.

4. In Luke 12:15, Jesus says, "Watch out! Be on your guard against all kinds of greed; life does not consist in an abundance of possessions." How might you connect this verse with the discussion about "keeping gifts in motion" and loving our neighbors as *they* need to be loved?

5. Consider the types of generosity reviewed in this chapter—and issues therein. What might make you more openhanded?

   a. spirit: spontaneous yes-ness

   b. speech: praise and listening, not flattery

c. time: *chronos* and *kairos*

d. possessions: identity and ownership

e. home: hospitality

f. receiving: givers giving

g. finances: frugality not stinginess

EXERCISE

1. Pair up with another person and find a significant difference in your personal history—experiences related to gender, ethnicity, money, health, etc. The exercise will be more fruitful if this difference is something that you believe influenced who you are today (such as divorce, a consistently supportive family, disease or death, a move that changed your outlook).

   As one person tells a story, the listener imagines what it might have been like to have this experience. Afterward, the listener repeats the story back—as compassionately as possible—until the storyteller is satisfied that the listener truly captured the emotions and issues expressed. Reverse roles.

   Discuss the experience of attempting to be empathetic and appreciative. In what ways did you imitate the attitude of Jesus in the incarnation? How might this practice—for you—influence the virtue of generosity?

9 ❧ SHOUTING SOFTLY

I have told you these things, so that in me you
may have peace. In this world you will have trouble.
But take heart! I have overcome the world.

JESUS, IN JOHN 16:33

When the Nazis rounded up Jews for extermination, a small percentage escaped into the forests of Europe. One such group—as told in the film *Defiance*—started out as a band of four brothers but eventually swelled to the size of a small town, about twelve hundred people. Resourceful, long-suffering and combat-savvy, they endured grim winters in Belarus and brutal assaults from the German army.

Early on, when helping to construct one of the forest shelters, a woefully unskilled "intellectual" dropped a wooden beam, nearly hitting the leader of the group, Tuvia Bielski. Tuvia reacted strongly, making the point that, to survive, everyone had to contribute on a practical level; everyone had to learn a specific skill. Later, the roles reversed, and the intellectual helped Tuvia see that a community also needed warm support and opportunities for artistic expression.

SURVIVAL IN THE WILDERNESS

I like this story because it shows how discipline, expertise and watchfulness are all crucial to making our way in the wilderness of this world. The forest may be stunningly beautiful—and well worth the effort hikers make—but there are significant threats, armies of temptation and winters of suffering. To contend with their enemies, everyone in the Bielski community committed themselves to learning what needed to be learned—becoming apprentices as necessary. And they combined their varied skills to build shelters. Even so, no matter how prepared or skilled the Bielski group was, they still might have been destroyed by the Nazis. Survival was not guaranteed. They needed God's mercy. So do we.

Becoming an apprentice. On Saturdays, I often learned home-repair skills from my dad. I enjoyed the smell of sawdust and the tangible results of my labor. One day, when using a band saw in the workshop, I pushed too hard and my thumb slipped into the blade. Blood spurted everywhere. Wincing, I pressed on the open cut, walked past my sister to the house and waited for her to open the door for me. As she strolled over without any urgency, I yelled, "What's taking so long? I'm bleeding to death!" She replied, "How was I supposed to know? You weren't screaming!" I resolved then and there always to raise my voice when in need.

But my dad said more to me than "Sorry you cut yourself." He said that my pushing hard on the wood should have told me that the saw blade was dull and that I needed to notice these types of things, both for my own safety and for the quality of the work I intended to produce.

When we accept that we are apprentices—novices learning under an accomplished tradesperson—several things follow. Most important, we submit to an experienced expert who is responsible to educate us. As disciples, apprentices in spiritual life, we could see Jesus as the Supreme Journeyman, a specialist at loving the Father, but also the Journey-man, the best guide for our travels. This second quality reminds us that the goal of living the quieter virtues is not to become virtuous for its own sake. It's to imitate Jesus as we walk alongside of him, to live in his presence as he would have us live. Unless we follow the God who transcends our experience, all we have is our experience.

Given the hazards of this world, we have a lot to learn from a wise leader, and this education will require of us "a long obedience in the same direction," as Eugene Peterson's book title states. Good habits require sustained repetition and informed coaching. We can count on Jesus' promise: "Students are not above their teacher, but all who are fully trained will be like their teacher" (Luke 6:40).

Building a shelter. A few months after the Tea Fire in Santa Barbara, the burned-out houses were bulldozed and the rebuilding began. After living next door to the construction, I can easily rank the most annoying power-tool noises (drywall drill and stucco hose!). But I can also attest to the skill with which these sophisticated shelters went up—in a coordinated effort from slab to framing, from roof to finished work. Likewise, Jesus-apprentices soon realize that one practice builds on another. As we find shelter in the Lord, we move from spiritual foundation and biblical framing to well-plumbed character and, ultimately, a welcoming landscape.

And so it is with the quieter virtues, as each one makes way for the next, a construction in keeping with Jesus' heavenly architecture. When discernment chooses between what is life-giving and what is life-threatening, it sees the wisdom of boundaries, a vision essential to innocence. As our innocence sets the good free and binds evil, we do justice to the truth about things, including the measure of authenticity inside us. The rigor of authenticity's inside-out consistency gives us the courage to accept a healthy modesty—and modesty's grasp of our emptiness prepares us for worship, so we kneel before the sacred and stand up to the profane. Living reverently before God develops the kind of trust that fosters contentment, for who can satisfy but God alone? And when we are truly content with what we have or do not have, we hold things loosely enough to live with the generosity of an open hand.

Though these steps imply one progression that is right and proper—or, at least, the most reasonable—other relationships can teach us as well. Reverence's "fear of God" could lead us to take more seriously the tasks of discernment presented to us in our culture. Generosity is other-centered in a way that might aid a modest assessment of our importance. A contentment not dependent on perfect circumstances might help us tell the truth in authentic ways. Virtue begets virtue—and in developing them we are sheltered under God's protection.

In the wilderness, a shelter makes survival possible, but so much more. Over time, as things improve, good shelters turn into good homes. We aren't just "getting by" and avoiding our enemies. We have the resources and energy to enjoy the beauty of the trees, the view from the ridge, the smell of fir needles underfoot, the golden hues and shadows of a sunset. Amazingly, over time, the Bielski group created a more thorough-going culture. They developed a hospital and a school. Musicians played and debaters argued. The place became a community of shelters.

SHOUTING SOFTLY

At times, our culture thrusts its wilder elements at us, acting like a bully, noisily proclaiming what seems too popular not to be true. Be entertaining! Make fun your highest priority! Flaunt whatever you've got! The problem isn't new. Summarizing the thoughts of a fourth-century theologian, Richard Foster says, "The strain of deadly thoughts seems so strong, so blatant, so loud, if you will. The godly virtues seem so weak, so unobtrusive, so quiet." Overwhelmed by these challenges, we may want to retreat into our shelter to pray.

But the quieter virtues shout softly. They provide a way to

live next to the neighborhood bully without becoming bullies ourselves—or reducing our voice to an intimidated whisper. In Dorothy L. Sayers's novel *Strong Poison*, the jurist Miss Climpson cast one of the few "not guilty" votes, creating a hung jury. She could stick to her convictions because "in a righteous cause, a little personal discomfort was a trifle, and . . . her religion had trained her to fasting." The quieter virtues shout softly, saying what needs to be said, in speech or other actions, because that's what we're called to do as apprentices.

Shouting softly is a way to think about giving voice to our commitments. Do we say, "Quieter virtues? Interesting material," and go our merry way? If you are at all like me, turning the last page of most books brings a sense of troubled pleasure. There's a feeling of accomplishment and a hope that comes from new ideas about how to make my way in the world. That's the pleasure part. The trouble comes when I think about all the ideas I haven't yet put into practice. I'm reminded of what I knew when I started. It's not more knowledge that I lack; it's more acting on the knowledge that I have. If I never learned one more thing about how to be an apprentice to the journeyman Jesus, I would still have a lifetime of ideas and principles and practices to apply. I know plenty to make my shelter less wobbly.

Maybe there's a principle of the universe here: the Inevitable Ratio of Limited Application. We have to listen to seventy-five hours of teaching for every twenty-five hours we actually apply. When the educational volume drops to seventy-four hours, our application falls off. It's as if new learning (or old reminding) must speak into our ears until it makes its way through our head and heart—and finally, as dependable habits, onto our lips and into our hands.

Perhaps each of us has a different ratio. For some, ninety-eight hours of listening is necessary to glean two hours of application. These folks go to conference after conference, attend seminars, listen to speakers, and read books and blogs and websites, but little gets spoken into their lives. Then again, some people apply almost everything they learn: fifty hours in means forty hours out. I wonder if Jesus was 1:99. From one teaching about love, he found an eternity of applications.

All of this is to say that being an apprentice always involves good listening. We *need* whatever it is *we* need to learn the quieter virtues. Eventually, we hope to give voice to what we've learned. We want the language of our lives to communicate God's beauty, to make a lovely sound, clear and resonant, to fill our shelters with fitting words and gestures, always fresh and inviting.

The quieter virtues speak into a wild and noisy world, shouting softly.

APPENDIX
definitions and disciplines*

Discernment is the *wisdom* to recognize the difference between life and death—with the motivation to choose life.

Discipline: Attentiveness (the stewardship of the present)

Innocence is our sense of *justice* that sets good things free and binds up evil.

Discipline: Advocacy (arguing for the good and against false accusers)

Authenticity is a rigorous inside-out consistency that *courageously* cares for others.

Discipline: Real presence (being fully, sincerely in the moment)

Modesty is gladly *tempering* the expression of our fullness with an understanding of our emptiness.

Discipline: Timely remembrance (turning our past into our teacher)

Reverence is, in *faith*, kneeling before the sacred and standing up to the profane.

---

*"Parent" (traditional) virtues are in italic.

Discipline: Astonishment (the willful appreciation for the miracle of the ordinary)

Contentment is the strength *hope* gives us to pursue the unsatisfied life in a satisfying way.

Discipline: Ars morendi (the art of dying well)

Generosity is the predisposition to *love* openhandedly.

Discipline: Compassionate imagination (imitating Christ's empathy and appreciation)

NOTES

Chapter 1: The Grinch Was Right

page 13 "something *feels* uniform": Todd Gitlin, *Media Unlimited: How the Torrent of Images and Sounds Overwhelms Our Lives* (New York: Owl Books, 2002), p. 7 (italics his).

page 14 "instead of doing everything": Carl Honoré, *In Praise of Slowness: How a Worldwide Movement Is Challenging the Cult of Speed* (San Francisco: Harper/SanFrancisco, 2004), p. 275. James Houston's words on the speed of character building are also insightful here: "If I think faster than I can speak, speak faster than I can act, act more than I have character to assimilate, there is already a basic disjunction within me, which challenges me to live a more integrated, authentic existence. But the extensions of forms and sensations that *techne* provides exacerbate our loss of integrity." *I Believe in the Creator* (Grand Rapids: Eerdmans, 1980), p. 27.

page 15 According to Oliver Sacks: *Seeing Voices: A Journey into the World of the Deaf* (Los Angeles: University of California Press, 1989), pp. 41-53.

page 19 "room for good": G. K. Chesterton, *Orthodoxy* (New York: Doubleday/Image, 1959), p. 95.

Chapter 2: Discernment

page 23 "How we spend our days": Annie Dillard, *The Writing Life* (New York: Harper & Row, 1989), p. 32.

pages 23-24 "What is REAL?": Margery Williams, *The Velveteen Rabbit: Or,*

How Toys Become Real (New York: Avon, 1975), p. 16.

page 24   "The issue isn't *can*": Thomas De Zengotita, *Mediated: How the Media Shapes Your World and the Way You Live in It* (New York: Bloomsbury, 2005), p. 21 (italics his).

page 25   "In fact we should never": C. S. Lewis, *Letters to Malcolm: Chiefly on Prayer* (New York: Harcourt Brace Jovanovich, 1964), p. 80 (italics his).

page 26   "newsak": Malcolm Muggeridge, *Christ and the Media* (Grand Rapids: Eerdmans, 1977), p. 37.

page 27   "Sight is free": Gabriel Josipovici, *Touch* (New Haven: Yale University Press, 1996), p. 9.

page 29   "Have thus succeeded": Ken Myers, *All God's Children and Blue Suede Shoes: Christians & Popular Culture* (Wheaton: Crossway Books, 1989), p. 18.

page 30   "the art of discovering": Merriam-Webster's Medical Dictionary, s.v. "physiognomy," <www.merriam-webster.com/medical/physiognomy>.

page 31   "Judgment is the most important": Oliver Sacks, *The Man Who Mistook His Wife for a Hat and Other Clinical Tales* (New York: Summit Books, 1985) p. 18.

page 33   "We cannot affirm": Tim Challis, *The Discipline of Spiritual Discernment* (Wheaton: Crossway Books, 2007), p. 102.

page 39   "Try to be one": Henry James, in *Bartlett's Familiar Quotations*, 16th ed., ed. Justin Kaplan (New York: Little, Brown, 1992), p. 548.

page 40   "attention is the commodity": Richard A. Lanham, *The Economics of Attention: Style and Substance in the Age of Information* (Chicago: University of Chicago Press, 2006), p. 12.

Chapter 3: Innocence

page 47   "second innocence": John Izzo, *Second Innocence: Rediscovering Joy and Wonder* (San Francisco: Berrett Koehler, 2004), p. 10.

page 47   "Children are innocent": G. K. Chesterton, quoted in J. R. R. Tolkien, *The Tolkien Reader* (New York: Ballantine, 1966), p. 44.

page 47   "not causing harm": Johannes P. Louw and Eugene A. Nida, eds., *Greek-English Lexicon of the New Testament: Based on Semantic Domains* (New York: United Bible Society, 1989), pp. 79, 88.

page 49   "What has happened to": Roger Shattuck, *Forbidden Knowledge: From Prometheus to Pornography* (New York: St. Martin's Press, 1996), p. 5.

page 52   "Experience . . . is": Dominic LaRusso, *Concepts and Skills of Oral Communication* (Cortona, Italy: Wm. Brown Publishers, 1973), pp. 52-53.

page 59   "Pepin: What is": J. I. Mombert, *A History of Charles the Great* (London: Kegan Paul, Trench, 1888), p. 245.

page 61   "He believed that 'decent'": Philip Hallie, *Lest Innocent Blood Be Shed: The Story of the Village of Le Chambon and How Goodness Happened There* (New York: HarperPerennial, 1979, 1994), p. 266.

Chapter 4: Authenticity

page 72   "I can define my identity": Charles Taylor, *The Ethics of Authenticity* (Cambridge, Mass.: Harvard University Press, 1991), p. 40.

page 74   "Grant that all": Plato, "Phaedrus," in *Readings in Classical Rhetoric,* ed. Thomas W. Benson and Michael H. Prosser (Davis, Calif.: Hermagoras Press, 1988), p. 41.

page 74   "pull the child": George MacDonald, *The Princess and Curdie* (New York: Penguin, 1966), p. 73.

page 76   "I am not a hypocrite": William Ian Miller, *Faking It* (New York: Cambridge University Press, 2003), p. 9.

page 76   "Let us pretend": C. S. Lewis, *Mere Christianity* (New York: Macmillan, 1960), p. 165.

page 78   "I can't die": Jack LaLanne, <www.revolutionhealth.com/pages/jack-lalanne--king-of-fitness->.

page 78   "Clothes do not make": Henry Ward Beecher, in *The International Thesaurus of Quotations,* trans. Rhoda Thomas Tripp,

(New York: Harper & Row, 1970), p. 164.

page 79   "in a media-conscious": Kiku Adatto, *Picture Perfect: The Art and Artifice of Public Image Making* (New York: Basic Books, 1993), p. 97.

page 80   "He recognized well enough": Charles Williams, *Descent into Hell* (Grand Rapids: Eerdmans, 1980), pp. 129-30.

page 82   "Biblical prayer is impertinent": Walter Wink, "Prayer and the Powers," *Sojourners*, October 1990, p. 13.

page 84   "the sole cause": Blaise Pascal, *Pensées*, trans. A. J. Krailsheimer (New York: Penguin, 1966), p. 67.

Chapter 5: Modesty

page 90   "that other people owe him": Joseph H. Kupfer, *Prostitutes, Musicians and Self-Respect: Virtues and Vices of Personal Life* (Lanham, Md.: Lexington Books, 2007), p. 22.

page 91   "entails looking outside": Harold Barrett, *Rhetoric and Civility: Human Development, Narcissism, and the Good Audience* (New York: SUNY Press, 1991), p. 41.

page 93   "To try to draw": Wendell Berry, *Sex, Economy, Freedom, and Community: Eight Essays* (New York: Pantheon Books, 1993), p. 141.

page 94   "power has displaced humility": Kari Konkola, "Have We Lost Humility?" *Humanitas* 18 (March 2005): 200.

page 96   "Those who are poor": George MacDonald, *Life Essential: The Hope of the Gospel* (Wheaton, Ill.: Harold Shaw, 1974), p. 44 (italics his).

page 96   "We are all frail": Thomas à Kempis, *The Imitation of Christ* (New York: Penguin, 1952), p. 29.

page 98   "Humility does not consist": Jeremy Taylor, in Richard Foster and James Bryan Smith, eds., *Devotional Classics: Selected Readings for Individuals and Groups* (San Francisco: HarperSanFrancisco, 1990), p. 269.

page 100   "When you hold": Jeremy Taylor, in ibid., p. 270.

page 102   Appearance is such a: For a compellingly argued treatment of sexual modesty, see Wendy Shalit, *A Return to Modesty: Discovering the Lost Virtue* (New York: Touchstone, 2000).

page 104   "how wisdom comes": Lois Lowry, *The Giver* (New York: Bantam Doubleday Dell, 1993), p. 78.

page 104   "Forgetting the past": Henri Nouwen, *The Living Reminder: Service and Prayer in Memory of Jesus Christ* (New York: Seabury Press, 1977), p. 22.

page 105   "I beg you": St. Augustine, *Confessions,* trans. R. S. Pine-Coffin (New York: Penguin, 1961), p. 247.

page 108   "the forfeited right": Aleksandr I. Solzhenitsyn, *A World Split Apart* (New York: Harper & Row, 1978), p. 25 (italics his).

Chapter 6: Reverence

page 111   "a rational response": Lawrence H. Davis, "The Importance of Reverence," *Faith and Philosophy* 7, no. 2 (1990): 142.

page 111   "the well-developed capacity": Paul Woodruff, *Reverence: Recovering a Forgotten Virtue* (New York: Oxford University Press, 2001), p. 8.

page 112   "Let my heart be broken": Bob Pierce, written on the flyleaf of his Bible, posted on World Vision's website <www.worldvision.in/&Our+History>.

page 114   "exclusive emphasis": Dan B. Allender and Tremper Longman, *The Cry of the Soul: How Our Emotions Reveal Our Deepest Questions About God* (Colorado Springs: NavPress, 1994), p. 100.

page 117   "Awe and reverence": J. Ben Patterson, ed., *Prayer Devotional Bible* (Grand Rapids: Zondervan, 2004), p. 1527.

page 118   "repetition would be a vulgarity": C. S. Lewis, *Perelandra* (New York: Macmillan, 1965), p. 43.

page 121   "The full fruitfulness": Thomas Merton, *No Man Is an Island* (New York: Harcourt Brace, 1955), p. 243.

page 121   "evil in the imagination": Frederick Buechner, *Telling the Truth: The Gospel as Tragedy, Comedy and Fairy Tale* (New York: Harper & Row, 1977), p. 7.

page 125   "the sacred intoxication": G. K. Chesterton, quoted in Frederick Buechner, *Speak What We Feel (Not What We Ought to Say): Reflections on Literature and Faith* (San Francisco: HarperSanFrancisco, 2001), p. 121.

page 125   "How can we contrive": G. K. Chesterton, *Orthodoxy* (New York: Doubleday/Image, 1959), p. 10.

page 128   "to be a witness": Abraham Heschel, in Victor Gross, *Educating for Reverence: The Legacy of Abraham Joshua Heschel* (Bristol, Conn.: Wyndham Hall Press, 1972), p. 74.

page 128   "It's strange how deserts": Terry Tempest Williams, *Refuge: An Unnatural History of Family and Place* (New York: Vintage, 1991), p. 148.

page 129   "Christ in distressing disguise": Mother Teresa, quoted in Malcolm Muggeridge, *Something Beautiful for God: Mother Teresa of Calcutta* (New York: Doubleday/Image, 1977), p. 72.

page 129   "God's image": Graham Greene, *The Power and the Glory* (New York: Penguin, 1990), p. 101.

Chapter 7: Contentment

page 135   "The deeper problems": Daniel Boorstin, *The Image: A Guide to Pseudo-Events in America* (New York: Atheneum, 1987), p. 211.

page 136   "the craving for salt": Frederick Buechner, *Wishful Thinking: A Theological ABC* (New York: Harper & Row, 1973), p. 54.

page 137   "Don't care how": <www.lyricsmania.com> (search under "Soundtrack Lyrics" for *Willy Wonka and the Chocolate Factory*).

page 137   "Greed has poisoned": Quoted on American Rhetoric: Movie Speech, *The Great Dictator* (1940) <www.americanrhetoric.com/MovieSpeeches/moviespeechthegreatdictator.html>.

page 138   "rotten with perfection": Kenneth Burke, *Language as Symbolic Action* (Berkeley: University of California Press, 1966), p. 16.

page 139   "complaint": Robert Kegan and Lisa Lahey, *How the Way We Talk Can Change the Way We Work: Seven Languages for Transformation* (New York: Jossey-Bass, 2001), p. 18.

pages 139-40   "To be discontented": Jeremiah Burroughs, *Rare Jewel of Chris-*

tian Contentment (Wilmington, Del.: Sovereign Grace, 2001), p. 73.

page 142   "Worry can": Jerry Sittser, *The Will of God as a Way of Life* (Grand Rapids: Zondervan, 2004), p. 135.

page 144   "Life is difficult": Scott Peck, *The Road Less Traveled* (New York: Simon & Schuster, 1978), p. 15.

pages 144-45 "We're all aware": Don DeLillo, *White Noise* (New York: Penguin, 1985), p. 288.

page 145   "being satisfied": Thomas Carson, "Happiness, Contentment and the Good Life," *Pacific Philosophical Quarterly* 62 (1981): 378.

page 145   "to accept 'what is'": Robert A. Johnson and Jerry M. Ruhl, *Contentment: A Way to True Happiness* (San Francisco: HarperSanFrancisco, 1999), p. x.

page 145   "easy to please": George MacDonald, in C. S. Lewis, *Mere Christianity* (New York: Macmillan, 1960), p. 172.

page 147   "Hope frees us": Henri J. M. Nouwen, *Here and Now: Living in the Spirit,* 10th ed. (New York: Crossroad, 2006), p. 37.

page 147   "a belief in a positive": Wikipedia, s.v. "Hope" <http://en.wikipedia.org/wiki/Hope>.

page 149   "full contentment": Westminster Shorter Catechism (1674), posted on Christian Classics Ethereal Library <www.ccel.org/creeds/westminster-shorter-cat.html>.

page 150   "My chief care": Thomas Merton, *Seeds of Contemplation* (Norfolk, Conn.: New Directions, 1949), p. 19.

page 151   "play freely": Stephen Nachmanovitch, *Free Play: Improvisation in Life and Art* (New York: Tarcher/Putnam, 1990), pp. 21-22.

page 153   "I must have my wants": Jeremiah Burroughs, *The Rare Jewel of Christian Contentment* (Wilmington, Del.: Sovereign Grace, 2001), p. 17.

Chapter 8: Generosity

page 160   "To speak of gifts": Lewis Hyde, *The Gift: Imagination and the*

Erotic Life of Property (New York: Vintage, 1983), p. 22.

page 160   "Love Can Be Kept": Thomas Merton, *No Man Is an Island* (New York: Harcourt Brace, 1983), p. 3.

page 164   "If we are going to": Ibid., p. 6.

page 164   "Each gift stays": Hyde, *The Gift*, p. 14.

page 166   "The prevalence of altruistic": Karl Sigmund, Ernst Fehr and Martin A. Nowak, "The Economics of Fair Play," *Scientific American*, January 2002, p. 87.

page 167   "There are people who": Keith Johnstone, *Impro: Improvisation and the Theatre* (New York: Routledge, 1987), p. 92 (italics mine).

page 169   "render the unspeakable": Walker Percy, "The Diagnostic Novel: On the Uses of Modern Fiction," *Harper's Magazine*, June 1986, p. 40.

page 172   "Every claim of ownership": Luke Johnson, *Sharing Possessions: Mandate of Symbol and Faith* (Philadelphia: Fortress, 1981), p. 40.

page 173   "Hospitality . . . requires": Henri Nouwen, *The Wounded Healer* (New York: Doubleday/Image, 1979), p. 89.

page 175   "keep discovering what": Bernard Häring, *The Virtues of an Authentic Life* (Liguori, Mo.: Liguori Press, 1997), p. 111.

page 177   "I don't try to get": G. K. Chesterton, *The Secret of Father Brown* (New York: Penguin, 1975), p. 13.

page 178   "The world is fairly": Annie Dillard, *Pilgrim at Tinker Creek* (New York: Harper & Row, 1985), p. 15.

Chapter 9: Shouting Softly

page 184   "The strain of deadly": Richard J. Foster and Gayle D. Beebe, *Longing for God: Seven Paths of Christian Devotion* (Downers Grove: IVP Books, 2009), p. 63.

page 185   "in a righteous cause": Dorothy L. Sayers, *Strong Poison* (New York: Avon, 1967), p. 33.

ABOUT THE AUTHOR

Gregory Spencer has been working as a writer since fourth grade, when he typed out a thirty-page short story about a collie and a magic eight-ball. This surefire career became sidetracked for decades when the story was thrown out by a family member who "helpfully cleaned out" his desk one day.

After college, he worked with InterVarsity's Twentyonehundred Productions for two years. Then, to his delight, he married Janet (his First Editor par excellence), and they were later graced with three daughters—Emily, Hannah and Laura, now in their twenties.

Greg is a professor of communication studies at Westmont College in Santa Barbara. He received his Ph.D. from the University of Oregon. His previous books are *A Heart for Truth: Taking Your Faith to College* (Baker) and two novels in the Three Dimensional Tale series: *The Welkening* (Howard) and *Guardian of the Veil* (Simon and Schuster/Howard). He's published numerous articles and poems. When not teaching (and grading!), writing or speaking, Greg might be found on the tennis court or in the garden.

For more information, see: www.gregory-spencer.com